ESSENTIAL MANAGEMENT
Checklists

ESSENTIAL
MANAGEMENT
Checklists

Jeffrey P Davidson

**Kogan
Page**

Dedication

This book is dedicated with love, to Shirley Davidson who, especially in the last nine years, really showed her stuff, and to Eileen Kelley, who took life's toughest punches but always came up smiling.

First published in the United States of America in 1986
by National Press Inc, 7508 Wisconsin Avenue, Bethesda, Maryland 20814.

Copyright © Jeffrey P Davidson 1986

This edition first published in Great Britain in 1987
by Kogan Page Ltd, 120 Pentonville Road, London N1 9JN.

New material copyright © Kogan Page Ltd 1987

British Library Cataloguing in Publication Data
Davidson, Jeffrey P.
 (Checklist management). Essential management
 checklists.
 1. Personnel management
 I. (Checklist management)   II. Title
 658.3   HF5549

 ISBN 1-85091-312-9
 ISBN 1-85091-416-8 Pbk

Typeset by Castlefield Press Ltd of Wellingborough
Printed and bound in Great Britain by Richard Clay Ltd, Bungay, Suffolk

Contents

Checklists

Figures in text

Part 1

Starting Off Right

Congratulations! You're now a manager. Whether you recently assumed this role, or have had it for a while you've quickly learned that every working day your staff count on you for direction, feedback, support and leadership. Any way you look at it, it's a large, potentially high-stress, seemingly never-ending task. And, to complicate matters further, your organisation, department or division asks more and more of you as you begin to have less time.

What can managers and supervisors do to assemble or develop a winning team that accomplishes assigned goals and objectives while working in unison and remaining friendly?

Read on!

In Starting Off Right, which comprises Chapters 1 to 8, we'll discuss how to assemble or develop an effective staff who can help to make both your job and theirs more enjoyable.

CHAPTER 1

So You're the Boss

The terms supervisor and manager are often used interchangeably. Perhaps the best description of the role of the supervisor is offered by William S Dinsmoor, that 'supervision involves overseeing one generally cohesive function, whereas management involves integrating and co-ordinating dissimilar functions that are related in having a common objective'. More precisely, a supervisor is one who tells people what to do and how to do it.

The supervisor directly oversees the work of one or more individual employees while also maintaining many of his or her own operating duties—all in connection with the performance of a single cohesive function. The manager is one 'who tells people in fairly specific terms what to accomplish and then counsels them to the extent necessary in their efforts to accomplish these objectives'. The manager integrates and coordinates numerous dissimilar functions which all contribute to the same goal or set of goals.

The information and recommendations presented in this book relate to both supervisors and managers.

What makes an effective manager/supervisor? Well, the list is endless. And the answer can be as diverse as the number of business executives and authors alive today. Here's a checklist of some key items:

Checklist 1

THE SUCCESSFUL MANAGER

Characteristics
- ☐ Shows flexibility in handling situations.
- ☐ Readily assumes responsibility.
- ☐ Maintains an even keel even during emergencies.
- ☐ Is energetic and generally in good health.
- ☐ Is receptive to different approaches and opinions of others.

☐ Adapts to new situations or accepts change.
☐ Maintains productivity even under poor conditions.
☐ Effectively juggles many tasks at the same time.
☐ Maintains proper perspective in approach to problems and handling staff.

Approach
☐ Accepts calculated risk.
☐ Examines problems from many angles.
☐ Identifies crucial elements of large tasks.
☐ Avoids getting bogged down by details.
☐ Incorporates new information and data quickly.
☐ Avoids management crisis by troubleshooting and preventative measures.
☐ Incorporates changes in technology or methods that will improve operations.

Communication
☐ Motivates staff to do their best.
☐ Anticipates reaction of others to new ideas and suggestions.
☐ Develops effective listening capability.
☐ Seeks cooperation with other departments/divisions.
☐ Maintains open channel with upper management.
☐ Allocates sufficient time for planning.
☐ Offers effective day-to-day coordination.
☐ Matches staff capabilities with appropriate tasks.
☐ Makes decisions with confidence.

Whew! Perhaps no one has ever completely mastered all the points listed in Checklist 1. Nevertheless it is useful as a guide or a model for which to strive.

All for you

The content and format of this chapter, as in all other chapters in this book, have been especially prepared for you, the modern manager. Numerous checklists are offered which can be readily applied as needed. Long-winded passages dwelling on supervisory theory have been virtually eliminated and replaced with quick, easy-to-digest information that you can apply immediately.

Chances are you will read through the whole book only once, but will need to refer to specific sections over and over again. To accommodate this need, chapters have been sliced up into convenient 'digestible' portions.

Let's turn now to Chapter 2, Identifying and Attracting Talent, to learn how an effective team can be assembled.

Identifying and Attracting Talent

One of the most important factors in the long-term success of an organisation is hiring the right people to begin with. There is no substitute for good employees, and while the supervisor's job will always require a multitude of activities, having the right people on board can release more time for you to devote to other areas. Regardless of the size of the organisation for which you work, the chances are you have some responsibility for identifying and attracting effective staff members.

This chapter will help you to answer these questions:

☐ What is a job description and how is it used?
☐ What are the key components of a job description?
☐ What items are contained on a good application form?
☐ Why should the effective supervisor always keep an eye out for new talent?
☐ What are some sources for attracting new talent?
☐ Why and how are box number advertisements used?

Job descriptions

Tom Hanlon was recently promoted to supervisor in the northwest sales office of a durable goods manufacturing company. Tom hadn't even been in the new position for two weeks when he received a memo indicating that his assistance was requested in developing a job description for the new staff position that had been created. It suddenly occured to Tom that, although he knew the operations of the department inside and out, he had never actually written a job description and was reluctant to admit to anyone that this was the case.

You might be asked to prepare a job description. The purpose of defining a job prior to recruiting is that it clarifies the type of person wanted, and also assists in writing classified advertisements or other copy to attract qualified job candidates.

The job description should include specific duties, and working conditions, and working relationships the employee will encounter. It should clearly identify the qualifications and skills, including education and experience, that prospective employees must have, as well as the behaviour expected on the job. It is also advisable to include personal characteristics that are desired and will be an aid to job performance (eg promptness, physical strength, desire for increased responsibilities). After the job description is written it should be circulated to the personnel office or to the supervisor's boss to determine if the description is appropriate. (See example on page 20.)

Although the job description should leave no doubt in an applicant's mind about the qualification for the job, it is important to remain flexible about job specifications. Remember, the 'ideal' employee exists only in one's mind. By being too demanding, you may cause your organisation to end up paying higher salaries or having to wait much longer for positions to be filled.

Many organisations operate with either inadequate job descriptions or none at all, but a well-constructed job description simplifies performance appraisals, helps to prevent supervisors from making judgements based on inadequate measurements and even helps orientate new workers.

Here's a list formulated by Larry G McDougle of Indiana University:

Checklist 2

KEY COMPONENTS OF A GOOD JOB DESCRIPTION

- ☐ Position, title and classification.
- ☐ Description of proposed duties and responsibilities. (Might include activities organised according to frequency.)
- ☐ List of skills and special knowledge necessary.
- ☐ Outline of working conditions, especially any that are out of the ordinary.
- ☐ Description of the type of supervision that the position requires and who gives it. Also, to what extent there is supervision of others.
- ☐ Qualifications: education and work experience.
- ☐ Full or part-time. Permanent or temporary.
  (*Continued at foot of page 18.*)

Figure 1

Job description (blank)

POSITION, TITLE, CLASSIFICATION ————————————

LOCATION ————————————————————

DESCRIPTION OF DUTIES ——————————————

WHY THIS VACANCY HAS OCCURRED ——————————

AUTHORITY & LIMITATIONS ————————————

WHO/WHAT THE JOB WILL EFFECT
(ie geography, department, market)

SUPPORT STAFF, RESOURCES ——————————————

REPORTS TO————————————————————

MINIMUM QUALIFICATIONS ——————————————

HOURS ——————————————————————————

☐ Salary grades. Allowances.
☐ Nature of contact with other groups, such as the general public, other departments or government officials.
☐ Type of personal judgement, initiative or resourcefulness required.

Figure 2

Employment opportunity

Transport Department
Equipment Management, Heavy Equipment Section
Construction House, Hanger Lane, Greenford UB6 9JN

Distribution Department
Division of Wholesale Operations, Warehouse Section
Construction House, Hanger Lane, Greenford UB6 9JN

Announcement No: 098400C

WE ARE ACCEPTING APPLICATIONS FOR THIS POSITION ON AN OPEN AND CONTINUOUS BASIS

THIS POSITION IS BEING ADVERTISED TO ESTABLISH AN ELIGIBLE LIST FOR CURRENT AND FUTURE VACANCIES

The Montgomery Company Transport and Distribution Departments are seeking applicants for the position of Mechanic II. The employee will be responsible for skilled mechanical work at the journeyman level in the maintenance and repair of complex automotive, material-handling and construction equipment, such as petrol and diesel motors, buses, tractors, bulldozers, graders, fork-lifts, conveyor systems and other equipment. Employee will work one of the following shifts to be assigned as needed: 7.30 am—4.00 pm; 3.30 pm—12.00 midnight; or 11.30 pm—8.00 am.

Figure 3

Job description

Positions available

	Position: **Export sales manager, Middle East**

POSITION LOCATION

WHO/WHAT THE JOB WILL EFFECT

Duties: Promotion of our products in the Middle East. Follow up on all enquiries. Direct clerical staff in expediting export correspondence, tender requests, credit collection. Supervise shipping details, export licences, customs declarations. Arrange preparation of foreign language technical manuals. Provide technical and consultant assistance and public relations. Supervise on-site equipment installation. Provide inventory of spare parts for local service stations. Maintain current information on import-export tariffs, licences and restrictions. Supervise duties of a secretary and an expeditor.

DESCRIPTION OF DUTIES

SUPPORT STAFF, RESOURCES

Requirements: Minimum five years' experience in audio visual, special effects, animation, film lab and/or related electronic systems, or
Previous experience in sales of Oxberry or related equipment overseas.
Knowledge of Middle East language is highly recommended (Arabic, Farsi and/or Turkish)
Travel to the territories of the Middle East

MINIMUM QUALIFI-CATIONS

RECOMMENDED QUALIFI-CATIONS

Hours: Full-time flexible

HOURS

SALARY

Salary: £20,000 per year
Report or send CV to
Management Recruitment, 1047 South-ampton Row, London WC1B 5AL for the attention of J H Pearce.

Note. This description might also have included: who to report to; why this vacancy has occurred; position authority and limitations.

The application form

Undoubtedly your organisation uses some type of job application form. The application form is one of the many tools the middle manager uses in evaluating job candidates. A good application form should at a minimum request the listed information:

Checklist 3

INFORMATION SOUGHT ON APPLICATION FORM

- ☐ Identifying information, such as name, address and telephone number.
- ☐ Physical characteristics, such as height, weight, and health, and physical limitations.
- ☐ Education, including specialised training, courses or seminars.
- ☐ Experience through at least the last three or four employers.
- ☐ References, at least two; more is better.
- ☐ Other interests, clubs, associations, community involvement.

In determining what information is to be collected on an application form, it is necessary to reach a middle ground between the information that is desired and needed, and what can be obtained effectively on a three to four page form. (See sample on figure 4, page 22.)

The application form should not be used as the sole basis for recruiting decisions. Its main usefulness is to provide information for checking references and to facilitate good interviewing.

Talent sources

In addition to newspaper advertisements, there are many other sources that can be considered when seeking qualified personnel:

Figure 4

Application for employment

NAME: ——————————————————————————

ADDRESS: ————————————————————————

HOME TELEPHONE: ————— BUSINESS TELEPHONE: ———

NATIONAL INSURANCE NUMBER: ———————————————

DATE OF BIRTH: ——————————————— AGE: ———

PLACE OF BIRTH: ——————— NATIONALITY: ————

SINGLE: ——— MARRIED/DIVORCED/SEPARATED: ————

WHAT IS YOUR HEIGHT? ——————————————————

WHAT IS YOUR WEIGHT
IN INDOOR CLOTHES? ————————————————

POSITION(S) applied for ——————————————————

Applying for Full-time ————— Part-time ————— Specify days and
hours if part-time ——————————————————————

Were you previously employed by us? ————— If yes, when? ———

How did you hear of us? ——————————————————

Date available for work ——————————— 19 ———

Education

SCHOOL, COLLEGE OR UNIVERSITY	FROM	TO	SUBJECTS PASSED, AT WHICH LEVEL, AND DATE

Previous employment

By whom employed and nature of business	From	To	Starting salary	Job description and reason for leaving. Salary on leaving

Please use additional paper if necessary.

Please list other experiences, skills or qualifications ————

Signature   Date

Checklist 4

SOURCES OF POTENTIAL EMPLOYEES

- ☐ Recommendations of present employees
- ☐ Professional and trade associations
- ☐ College careers offices
- ☐ Employment agencies
- ☐ Previous employees
- ☐ Customers and suppliers
- ☐ Competitors' employees

Curriculum vitae exchanges with other departments and non-competing organisations, depending on the nature of the work to be done, and the following sources, should not be overlooked:

- ☐ Mental health organisations
- ☐ Vocational consultants
- ☐ Trade and technical schools
- ☐ Handicapped workers' associations

When seeking qualified part-time help, all the above sources should be considered, as well as the following:

- ☐ Temporary employment agencies which may prove to be far less expensive than adding permanent employees.
- ☐ Sandwich students.

Temporary manpower services can offer a large number of labourers. In many cases a good temporary worker will become a good full-time employee.

Using a box number

Use of a box number in the classified section of the newspaper is one way to obtain CVs for various positions without publicising the name of your company. It is particularly advantageous to use box number advertisements when it is suspected that an employee in a crucial position may be leaving. The advertisement can be coded to identify the publication it appeared in, or the date of the publication. For example 'Box 606T5Pr' could signify that envelopes received are responding to an ad placed in *The Times* on the fifth day of the month, for the production department.

At least twice a year an attempt should be made to evaluate the relative merits of the various sources of personnel through objective measurement. A table can be developed which compares turnover, grievances and disciplinary action, for example, with the recruiting sources. Such comparisons and tabulations, while not conclusive because of many other factors, can give valuable information in areas that may otherwise be difficult to assess objectively.

Now let's examine interviewing and reference checking in Chapters 3 and 4.

CHAPTER 3

Interviewing Made Easier

Jane Milner had recently been appointed as director of administration for an advertising and public relations agency. In her new position, Jane was responsible for interviewing job candidates. She was fairly confident that she could effectively conduct a 30–45 minute interview with any prospect who came through her door, and thus didn't feel the need to prepare questions in advance, or to undertake any preparation for that matter.

Five weeks to the day after she was hired, Jane had responsibility for interviewing candidates for a new position that had opened up with the agency. It took Jane only 45 minutes — the length of the first interview she conducted — to realise that preparation was indeed necessary. The interview was a shambles, Jane was nervous, lost track of what she was telling the prospect, and represented the agency poorly.

In this chapter we'll examine practical methods for preparing and conducting interviews. We'll also focus on the following questions:

☐ What should be done before the applicant arrives?
☐ What is a question funnel?
☐ When should the applicant be rated?
☐ What steps should you take following the interview?

Get ready, get set

Before the applicant arrives, plans should be made to structure the interview. It should be decided in advance what the objectives are, such as whether someone is wanted with long-range potential or growth potential. The job description will provide guidelines as to what the objectives of the interview should be. It is also important for the supervisor to know the position thoroughly and be able to describe the qualities that are essential for successful performance.

Attempt to create a 'question funnel' which involves beginning

Figure 5

INTERVIEW RATING										
POSITION APPLIED FOR			**NAME**							
DEPARTMENT			**ADDRESS**							
			TOWN				**POSTCODE**			
			PHONE							
AREA			**RATING**							
INTERPERSONAL SKILLS	1	2	3	4	5	6	7	8	9	10
ARTICULATION	1	2	3	4	5	6	7	8	9	10
APPEARANCE	1	2	3	4	5	6	7	8	9	10
POISE	1	2	3	4	5	6	7	8	9	10
AMBITION	1	2	3	4	5	6	7	8	9	10
EXPERIENCE	1	2	3	4	5	6	7	8	9	10
EDUCATION	1	2	3	4	5	6	7	8	9	10
SPECIAL TRAINING	1	2	3	4	5	6	7	8	9	10
OVERALL QUALIFICATIONS	1	2	3	4	5	6	7	8	9	10

Comments ——————————————————————
————————————————————————————————
————————————————————————————————
————————————————————————————————
————————————————————————————————

DATE   REVIEWER

with broad relevant questions, working towards the specific. To build trust, always pose a positive question before a negative one. The phrasing of questions should not be threatening. If you must probe for details, stick to 'echoing', which is making a question out of the applicant's last statement, or use the neutral 'tell me more' question.

A strong attempt should be made to be consistent with each candidate, in order that comparison with other candidates will be valid. Notes should be taken during the interview, but not during tense moments. For a good interview, the questions should be well-planned and there should be a true interest in what the applicant says.

Immediately following the interview, rate the applicant objectively. The rating can be as simple as below average, average, above average for abilities, training or traits that are essential for the position. Many interviewers use a 1 to 6, or a 1 to 10 scale to rate applicants. The method used for rating can vary; what is important is that criteria essential for the position are used and that the method for rating is as objective as possible.

The following interview questions are presented as a handy guide:

Checklist 5

INTERVIEW QUESTIONS

Accomplishment and goals

- [ ] How do you deal with people most effectively?
- [ ] What new skills or experience would you like to acquire in the immediate future?
- [ ] Cite your latest major career achievement?
- [ ] What problems have you solved that were plaguing your organisation?
- [ ] What do you do best?
- [ ] What do you prefer to do?
- [ ] Why are you seeking to change jobs? Or, what type of job are you applying for?
- [ ] Do you prefer long-term assignments or short assignments with quick feedback?
- [ ] How do you feel you could best contribute here?
- [ ] What leadership have you assumed in the past?

Education

- [ ] Why did you choose the school that you went to?
- [ ] What were your favourite/least favourite lessons?

☐ What level of effort was needed to achieve your results?
☐ What special projects or independent studies did you undertake?
☐ What courses you would like to take in the future?
☐ Looking back, would you choose the same school and subjects?
☐ What was your average position in class?

General

☐ Do you have any involvement in community organisations?
☐ What are your hobbies/interests?
☐ What would others say about your work or work habits?
☐ How well do you take constructive criticism?
☐ Do you get frustrated occasionally or do you tend usually to stay calm?
☐ What do you know about our company?
☐ In a sentence, why are you the best candidate for the position?

What if you're undecided about a candidate?

Now, here's another job interview checklist of tough questions from William A Cohen, author of *The Executive's Guide to Finding a Superior Job*.

This checklist is useful if you're undecided about a particular applicant or if the job to be filled requires a very special person.

Checklist 6

TOUGH QUESTIONS TO ASK A JOB CANDIDATE

☐ What's wrong with your present job?
☐ Does your boss know you are looking for a job?
☐ Why have you made so many job changes?
☐ Why are you interested in our company?
☐ How ambitious are you?
☐ What are your three greatest strengths, in order?
☐ What are your three greatest weaknesses, in order?
☐ Where do you want to be in five years?
☐ Where do you think you'll be?

- ☐ Are you technically or management orientated?
- ☐ Do you feel you have top management potential? Why?
- ☐ How good a worker are you? Details?
- ☐ How good a leader are you? Details?
- ☐ What have you disliked most about past jobs?
- ☐ What do you think you would like best about this job?
- ☐ How important to you is salary compared to other aspects of the job?
- ☐ What does the word success mean to you?
- ☐ What type of job are you looking for?
- ☐ Why aren't you making more money?
- ☐ Why should we be interested in engaging you?

Who's looking for a job

It is helpful to know why the applicants are seeking a position with your organisation. Some applicants may have left their former job because they could not get along with the boss. They will not mention this immediately, because they feel it will make them look bad. Rather than criticise their former boss, they will cite differences of policy or principle. If additional questioning reveals that they simply did not get along with their boss, do not downgrade the applicant for not admitting that; few will. This individual may do a good job.

Often one encounters applicants who have been in many organisations—none of them for long. This may indicate personality problems, lack of direction, or simply a sustained avoidance of responsibility and hard work. It is best to stay away from applicants who have had several positions of short duration. Also avoid applicants who stress who they know rather than what they have accomplished or are able to accomplish.

An applicant who has done his or her homework; someone who knows about the company or your department, as strategist Pete R Johnson advocates, or has taken the time to assess what your needs may be, should be given extra consideration. Many applicants, in essence, are asking, 'What do you have for me?' Thus, it is refreshing to encounter an applicant who says, 'This is how I can contribute,' or 'Here is where I think I can benefit the organisation.'

Reasons for not recruiting

Discussion with supervisors, personnel managers and others with recruiting responsibilities reveals many common factors why applicants are not hired. Often the key reason stems from one of the following:

Checklist 7

REASONS FOR NOT RECRUITING

☐ The personal 'chemistry' between applicant and interviewer was not right.

☐ The applicant has had too many jobs without accompanying upward movement.

☐ An agreement on salary could not be reached.

☐ A reference check revealed that the applicant had a poor employment record.

☐ The applicant interviewed poorly.

Other reasons that were cited less often include the applicant not having 'the right background' or not seeming to have 'sufficient growth potential'.

But beware, the criteria you use to hire new employees may be irrelevant and could actually produce an inferior workforce. Analysis of extensive interviews over many years (in the US)* has shown that 'external qualities so long used as "knock-out" or selection factors do not hold up' as reliable employment evaluators.

The indication is that experience has as little to do with eventual success on the job as sex, age, race, formal education and the other items mentioned above. 'How often is ten years' experience simply one year's *bad* experience repeated ten times?' This study turned up an abundance of repeated bad experiences . . . apparently, failures by supervisors and their employees to correct past mistakes.

What counts are the dynamics within a human being that make him or her appropriate or not appropriate for a particular job,' according to the researchers. 'If industry will match an individual's personality to the real requirements of the job . . . increased productivity, reduced turnover, and better job satisfaction can be assured.'

Interview follow-up

As a follow-up to the initial interview the following recommendations are made for applicants for which there is strong interest:

*Herbert and Jeanne Greenberg, Personality Dynamics Inc.

☐ Make a reference check (see page 34).

☐ When possible, arrange a second interview and have other employees interview applicants.

No one should be engaged on the spot; wait a while so that the applicant has adequate time to consider the situation and an increased measure of objectivity can be gained during that time.

After interviewing a strong candidate for an open position, it is a good idea to have the job candidate formulate his or her own job description based on what he or she has learned about the job. At a second interview, review the candidate's job description and compare it with your original description. If the differences in the job description interpretations are mutually resolved (given that all other factors have been considered), an offer/no-offer decision can be made.

In the next chapter we'll examine the oh, so important responsibility of checking references.

CHAPTER 4
Checking References

The need to check references of job applicants is becoming increasingly apparent. As discussed in Chapter 6, Spotting Fake CVs, more than a few of the job applicants that you'll encounter will misrepresent themselves in some way on their curricula vitae or application forms.

in touch with the references offered by job applicants because a substantial body of useful information on the applicant can be gleaned quickly. This chapter will show how to check references effectively and verify other information submitted by applicants. We'll also provide answers to the following questions:

- ☐ Why is it better to phone rather than write to referees?
- ☐ How can you quickly gain the information you need to help assess the suitability of job applicants?
- ☐ What type of conversational tone is best to obtain useful information from a previous employer?
- ☐ What does a long-winded, uninformative answer to one of your questions often mean?
- ☐ Why should references beyond those listed by the applicant be sought?

Using the phone

You've interviewed someone who seems just right for the job. But, you recognise that it's still important and revealing to make a reference check. If at all possible, make telephone reference checks rather than seeking information by post. Why? Because more information can be obtained in a shorter time by phone. Few people are willing to put negative comments on paper. Also, voice cues are extremely helpful.

When phoning referees speak slowly and assuredly, offering your name, position and company and the reason you're calling: 'John Smith has given us your name as a reference.'

If you have a checklist to work from, your time and effectiveness on the telephone will be greatly enhanced. (See Checklist 9.)

What to ask

Listed below are 15 points which will enable you to gain a wealth of information on job applicants.

1. *Employment dates*. What are the exact dates of the applicant's employment with your organisation/company/department/firm?
2. *Initial job*. What were the applicant's initial responsibilities when starting work with you?
3. *Ending job*. What were the applicant's current or last responsibilities on the job?
4. *Supervisory need*. What level of supervision did the applicant require?
5. *Team member*. Did the applicant prefer to work as part of a team or on his or her own?
6. *Conflicts encountered*. What work/job/career related conflicts did the applicant encounter?
7. *Attendance/absenteeism*. What was the applicant's record of attendance?
8. *Strengths*. Can you cite three to five of the applicant's strengths?
9. *Weaknesses*. Can you cite three to five of the applicant's weaknesses?
10. *Learning capability*. Does the applicant possess quick learning ability? If not, adequate learning ability?
11. *Record compared with others*. What is the applicant's record compared with others, i.e. such as colleagues and those with similar duties or responsibilities?
12. *Why leaving*. Based on your knowledge, why did the applicant depart (or why is the applicant leaving) your organisation?
13. *How replaced*. How will you replace the applicant upon his or her departure?
14. *Parting salary*. What is the final salary earned by the applicant in your organisation?
15. *Would you re-engage?* Given your experience with the applicant and in recognition of job requirements, would you re-engage the applicant?

In addition, here are other questions you may wish to pose to referees which will shed even more light on a job applicant's capabilities and suitability for the position available with you.

Checklist 8

OTHER QUESTIONS TO ASK REFEREES

- ☐ Could you please rank the applicant's responsibilities in descending order?
- ☐ What is the best way to work with the applicant for his or her greatest effectiveness and output?
- ☐ What could the applicant have done to be more successful?
- ☐ How would you describe the applicant's overall attitude?
- ☐ What additional training, courses, or activity does the applicant need for continued development?

Listen between the lines

An increase in litigation has made former employers cautious of saying anything negative about former employees. Thus it is of great importance to 'listen between the lines'; rely on your own instincts of what the reference is really telling you. For example, less than glowing praise regarding an applicant's record compared with others may well mean the applicant is mediocre. The same holds true for a long-winded response that really doesn't answer your question. Less than an immediate 'yes' to the question 'Would you re-engage this person?' can well mean 'no'.

Checklist 9

TELEPHONE REFERENCE CHECKLIST

APPLICANT'S NAME ——————— REFEREE NAME ————————

STREET ———————————— TITLE ————————————

TOWN ————————————— COMPANY ——————————

POSTCODE ——————————— STREET ————————————

PHONE NUMBER ——————— TOWN ————————————

POSTCODE————————

DATE———————————————— PHONE NUMBER———————

35

1. Employment dates —————————————————————

2. Initial responsibilities—————————————————

3. Ending responsibilities —————————————————

4. Supervisory needs —————————————————————

5. Team member—————————————————————————

6. Conflicts encountered—————————————————

7. Attendance/absenteeism —————————————————

8. Strengths (3–5) —————————————————————

9. Weaknesses (3–5) ————————————————————

10. Learning capability —————————————————————

11. Record compared with others —————————————

12. Why leaving? ————————————————————————

13. How replaced? —————————————————————

14. Parting salary ———————————————————————

15. Would you re-engage? —————————————————

You may find that some Personnel Departments will not give telephone references without proof of your bona fides, so it may be necessary to write, then phone (ostensibly to check the written reference, but really to supplement the information by personal conversation).

If you can't phone, write

It's likely that you can't get nearly the same amount of information by writing as by phoning for several reasons:

1. No one likes to take the time to write the responses to your questions;
2. No one likes to put negative reports in writing;
3. Writing provides no voice cues.

If you have trouble contacting a reference by phone, Checklist 10 can be used. Note particularly the comments section as some may be offered in the case of outstanding employees.

Remember that many referees have built-in biases. Some people have very little good to say about anyone. Some employers resent the fact that the employee left them. Still others always generalise when asked specifically about someone else's performance.

To get the most mileage out of a reference check, particularly if it's the applicant's previous employer, it's essential to establish a cordial, vibrant conversation.

Checklist 10

WRITTEN REFERENCES

_____   _____

_____   DATE

_____   RE: EVALUATION OF

_____   _____

Dear _____

We are at present in the process of evaluating many candidates for the position of _____ in our
_____ office.

To help us in the selection process and also to benefit the individual chosen, could you please take a few minutes to assess _____

37

objectively, based on your first-hand experience in working with him or her. For your convenience you may return this letter. Thank you for your cooperation.

Yours sincerely

	(lowest)							(highest)	
	1	2	3	4	5	6	7	8	9	10
energy, enthusiasm									
output, productivity									
dependability									
ability to handle pressure									
attendance/ punctuality									
learning capability									
overall value to organisation									

COMMENTS ———————————————————————

————————————————————————————————————

————————————————————————————————————

The extra effort

In addition to checking the references submitted by the applicant, make the extra effort to get in touch with the applicant's former bosses or supervisors, co-workers, and others who may not have been listed as references but can offer very revealing information.

A recurrent theme

It's a recurrent theme throughout this book that management/super-vision and employee communications is a dynamic process and the coming and going of employees is a continuous process. Checking references is thus a mandatory function of the candidate selection process, as it clearly increases the probability of recruiting capable, responsible employees.

When possible, arrange a second interview with the applicant, particularly after references have been checked, to get a more rounded, objective view of the applicant.

No one should ever be engaged on the spot, even if it's a second interview and all the references have responded marvellously. As a professional courtesy, one to two weeks' consideration time should always be offered.

Checklist 11

CHECKING REFERENCES

- ☐ Make telephone reference checks rather than seeking information by post.
- ☐ Work from a prepared telephone reference checklist.
- ☐ Listen between the lines of what the referee is telling you.
- ☐ Use a postal reference check when you have trouble contacting a reference by phone.
- ☐ Make an extra effort to get in touch with the applicant's former bosses, supervisors etc.
- ☐ Do not engage anyone on the spot. Offer one to two weeks' consideration time.

CHAPTER 5
Acknowledging Built-in Turnover Factors

Walter Ross had always prided himself on his ability to assist in the selection of the right type of worker for his department. When a recent job opening developed, Walter carefully reassessed the skills and abilities necessary to handle the position successfully. Walter was instrumental in the selection of Harry Morris, who would be handling some key accounts.

In the weeks that followed Harry made reasonable progress, yet did not seem particularly happy in his new position. One morning Harry approached Walter and told him that 'things just weren't working out'. He then promptly resigned. Walter was stunned. Yet with a little more research into Harry's recent job experience the situation might have been avoided.

In this chapter we'll answer the questions:

☐ Why do so many new recruits leave after only a short time in the job?
☐ What are five potential built-in turnover factors that can be spotted early?
☐ What type of employee generally requires a more structured organisation?
☐ How will knowing potential built-in causes of staff loss help to reduce overall turnover?

A mass exodus

Why do so many recruits with seemingly adequate or even superior capabilities leave in less than a year (and too often in a matter of months)? Frequently the reason is that one of several factors that all but guaranteed a rapid departure existed at the outset.

Checklist 12

BUILT-IN TURNOVER FACTORS

Even if the selection process goes well and it appears that a good position to job candidate has been made, there may be trouble in the coming months if any one of the following circumstances is present:

☐ Someone is hired for a lower salary than he or she previously achieved.

☐ A new employee has no supervisory responsibilities but did previously.

☐ The position does not represent forward movement for the new employee.

☐ The new employee requires a highly structured, organisational setting, or

☐ A clear, mutual understanding of job responsibilities was never established.

Let's examine these five so-called built-in turnover factors.

Engaged at a lower salary

An employee recruited for less money, or the same that he or she made previously often spells trouble. No one likes to work for less than they made before and, given the creeping, if not relentless increase in the cost of living, earning the same amount that you made before is also working for less.

An employee who takes a job at a lower salary will soon become unhappy as he or she sees his purchasing power decline. Moreover, an employee who takes such a job may be merely taking a position for the quick cash that can be generated, while continuing to seek a position for greater rewards. Generally, it is not recommended to take on someone who is willing to accept a salary that is less than or equal to what they have made previously.

No supervisory responsibilities

A new employee who has no supervisory responsibilities, but formerly had them, may soon feel frustrated. If an employee is taken on who previously managed a department of 10 to 12 people, for example, and is now joining your company as a staff person with authority over no one else, it won't be long before this individual misses the responsibility and control that had been attained in the previous job. (Unless, of course, in a previous position he or she disliked managing others or is semi-retired and not interested in shouldering heavy responsibilities.)

No forward movement

If the position does not represent a move upwards or a new career for the new employee—again, problems may soon develop. If the employee accepts a position with your business that represents a sideways move, you may later find that you have taken on someone who intends to 'coast' or 'retire' on the job; we have come to expect that most career-minded individuals seek at least a slightly better job than the one that they previously held.

Structured position required

Some employees require a highly structured position in an organisational network. For example, it is difficult for some individuals to move from a large corporation to a small firm. In a large corporation there were systems and procedures to be followed for every facet of operations. In the smaller firm, the red tape, corporate procedure and paper shuffling may be less.

Many employees who previously worked in larger corporate settings found comfort in the systems and paper work and, surprisingly, will not function as effectively in a more loosely structured business environment. In addition, the larger organisation had a fully established network and hierarchy of positions through which the employee could fully understand how he or she fitted into the organisational network. In a smaller organisation this may not be clear and may be unsettling to some employees.

Mutual understanding not established

Many new recruits leave a company because the job turned out to be something entirely different from what he or she originally had conceived. This has to be the responsibility of the interviewers and managers/supervisors who initiated the recruitment in the first place.

Conclusion

There are literally hundreds of reasons why new employees don't work out. The five discussed in this chapter provide a base or frame of reference from which you, as supervisor, can begin to alleviate the turnover problem.

In the next chapter we'll focus on the increasing evidence of faked CVs and how to avoid recruiting someone who uses one!

Later, in Part 6, we'll examine how to handle the departure of good employees.

CHAPTER 6

Spotting Fake CVs

Faked CVs, or at least those that contain misrepresentations, are nothing new to the working world, but in times of economic fluctuation appear with increasing frequency. It is said that nearly 80 per cent of all CVs contain at least some misleading information, usually in the area of employment history. 'The most common misrepresentation occurs when candidates fabricate names of firms they worked for to cover long gaps of unemployment.'

This chapter will focus on these key areas:

☐ Why do more and more applicants make false claims or misrepresentations on their CVs?

☐ Why are no gaps in an individual's employment record a possible clue to misrepresentation?

☐ How can school attendance and courses be inflated on the CV?

☐ Why should you be wary of achievements stated in non-specific terminology?

☐ How can you quickly verify CV information during the interview?

A frequent phenomenon

Selecting the right job applicant for a position can be a costly and time-consuming process. As the number of CVs or job applicants increases dramatically compared with the number of advertised job openings, applicants are naturally eager to present themselves via a covering letter and CV in the best possible way. Knowing that competition is keen, many resort to 'improving' their CVs through misrepresentation, fabrication and outright fraud.

Supervisors, personnel officers and top management from large organisations to the very smallest are generally aware of the faked CV phenomenon. However, few interviewers have the time to verify an applicant's CV fully, and when verification is done, it consumes time and money. Let's examine some ways to spot a faked CV or, at least, to alert oneself to its possibility, thus conserving resources and enhancing movement towards the selection of the best bona fide job applicant.

No employment gaps

For entry level for job applicants as well as for more senior individuals with at least five to seven years of employment experience, the odds are that there has been some unemployment or down time. A CV which indicates an airtight chronological sequence of employment with no gaps is actually the exception rather than the rule these days. One familiar technique used by many applicants is to offer job histories by years rather than by month and year. This, of course, affords one the opportunity to disguise as much as 12 months or more of unemployment or other activity. Similarly, individuals who have been self-employed, worked in a family-owned business or had a previous employer who subsequently went out of business are afforded an opportunity to arrange the dates of their employment history creatively.

Citing colleges but not the type of degree

Now and then a CV may cross your desk in which a job applicant has cited the name of the university he or she attended without accompanying information as to the type of degree or major subject area. If one is to meet this individual the remedy is, of course, to ask for this additional information and, even better, to ask for documentary proof.

Often, when phonies set out to prepare a CV, they go for the best, or at least what they perceive to be the best, or what they perceive will get them the furthest, citing good degrees from good universities. Again, a request for proof settles all.

Inflating specialised courses

Related to the issue of not fully identifying one's educational background is the rather common practice of inflating specialised courses taken to make it appear that one attended a particular university for four full years or for a full graduate programme. The MBA or graduate business school programme of some universities now offers executive development programmes or project management and marketing programmes which require six to eight weeks of intensive study. Generally, these are excellent. Often, however, graduations from these limited programmes are conveyed on some individuals' CVs as if the course work involved much more or yielded a graduate or undergraduate degree rather than just a certificate.

Many CV preparers who have attended but one summer, adult, weekend, or extension course of a major university present such on the personal history as 'attended University of _____'. This too is outright misrepresentation.

Citing achievements with broad-based numerical ranges

Have you ever examined the CV that included phrases such as the following:

— 'saved the company over £100,000 . . .'
— 'did 100 per cent over quota . . .'
— 'increased market share by more than 15 per cent . . .'

Any one of the above constitutes a lofty achievement, and there is no reason why the individual citing such an achievement could not give more specific figures. As a rule of thumb, terminology such as more than, over than, greater than, rather than the precise figure is a signal that exaggeration and misrepresentation may be occurring.

A problem here to stay

It's not likely that the incidence of fake CV preparation is likely to decrease in the near future. Moreover, even if you're a pro at spotting what appears to be a misrepresentative CV, undoubtedly more than a few will slip by you without being detected. While it's far more costly and time-consuming to conduct an interview with a job applicant than to simply review or read his or her application, in terms of verifying CV information it's far easier during an interview.

To verify educational background data with fairly recent college graduates, you might try the following: 'I see you went to X University. Were you there when Professor Adams headed your school?' The truthful applicant will state the name of the Professor who served while he or she attended that university. The phony will hum and haw, state that he or she can't remember or provide some other vague response such as 'I think so', 'I'm not sure' or 'I'll have to check'. If you doubt that asking for the name of one's college Professor is not a fair test, pose the question to your junior staff members or colleagues and you'll quickly see that most or all are readily able to recall the name.

The award winning candidate

Another ploy of phonies is to create a list of awards and honours that they've received or to cite various publications. The easiest way to confirm this information is to request documentation or copies of such items while on the phone with the applicant to arrange the interview. Here again, an applicant who has truly won such and such awards or had articles published in various journals will be able to supply documentation and will do so gladly. The phony may become uneasy when such requests are made during the initial phone call and will undoubtedly have an excuse during the interview as to why the materials could not be produced.

I have never met an individual who, having written a published article and listed it on his or her CV, was not readily able to supply me with at least a photocopy.

While it's not always possible to spot a fake CV, steps can be taken to ensure that the number of faked CVs received is reduced. Many organisations have stated their policy regarding fraud or misrepresentation on job application forms. One could even make reference to this policy in newspaper employment advertisements. Finally, the policy could be simply stated in a clause or paragraph which accompanies all correspondence with new job applicants.

If some of the items discussed above seem like added burdens, then consider the added burden to you and your organisation when you recruit the wrong person for the job based partially on the fake CV that he or she submitted.

Here's a checklist for quickly vetting that 'too good to be true' CV:

Checklist 13

CHECKING UP ON A CV

☐ Are there gaps in employment? This is very probable these days.

☐ Are schools and universities cited with no mention of degree earned? Maybe he or she never got one.

☐ Does the candidate seem to have a phenomenal educational background? It could be a case of inflated specialised courses.

☐ Are achievements cited with glossover terminology, such as 'saved more than'?

☐ Can the applicant name specific people from his or her past such as the head of the department, or editor of the journal in which he or she was published?

☐ Can the applicant provide documentation regarding awards received or articles published?

In the next chapter we'll examine applicants' CVs even more closely— not for misrepresentation—but for tell-tale signs that may signal disqualification.

CHAPTER 7

Reading Between the Lines of CVs

Curricula vitae are designed to contain useful information concerning the qualifications of job applicants. By carefully examining them further, however, one can gain valuable clues indicating which applicants should be disqualified beyond those that have used outright misrepresentation. The job of selecting the most qualified applicant for a position is never easy. Being able to remove marginal applicants from consideration quickly will, at the very least, enhance the selection process.

This chapter discusses six techniques for 'reading between the lines' of a CV and answers these questions:

- ☐ What can the quality of the copy of CV tell you about the applicant?
- ☐ Is a long list of outside hobbies and interests helpful or harmful for future performance?
- ☐ Does use of non-traditional sized or coloured paper yield important information?
- ☐ What type of stationery used should automatically disqualify a job applicant?
- ☐ Why, unfortunately, is it often necessary to eliminate many applicants quickly via clues from the CV?

A copy of a copy

There's nothing wrong in particular about a CV that has been photocopied. With the wide installation of high speed quality copiers more and more people are using photocopiers. A warning buzzer should go off, however, when you examine a CV that appears to be a second or third generation photocopy, or a 'copy of a copy'. If a job applicant and potential employee will submit a CV that has a poor appearance or is shoddy, it is likely that when hired he or she will take short-cuts on the job.

Many believe that disqualifying an applicant for sending a copy of a copy is too stern a measure. However, the image that one conveys, especially via written correspondence, is important and undoubtedly will provide clues as to future behaviour.

Over-listing of outside activities

There's nothing necessarily wrong with someone who belongs to a wide variety of civic, professional, recreational and social groups. An over-listing of these types of activity, however, may indicate that the person is a 'joiner' and not a 'doer'. Someone who is over-engaged in outside activities may be providing an indication that, once hired, he or she will provide only a minimum of effort on the job.

One other potential problem with an individual who has over-listed activities is that he or she may lack the ability to focus attention on specific areas of interest. This section of the CV must be examined closely since there is a fine line between an active, industrious person and an overbooked socialite.

Ambiguous dates in employment history

It's no longer a business or professional stigma to have a gap in employment dates. Gaps represent the rule rather than the exception. A problem exists when a CV contains ambiguous information regarding the dates of the applicant's employment. Be wary of a CV that contains only yearly information and not month and year, or if the timing of the transition from one job to the next is so smooth as to possibly be contrived.

An over-long CV

An over-long CV, especially one that contains a long list of achievements, could spell trouble. On paper, it's easy enough to beef up anything anyone has ever done. When reviewing awards or achievements cited, focus more on quality—what was accomplished, for whom and in what time—rather than quantity of items listed. Also, keep in mind that the industry and company from which an applicant came may have been in the habit of making periodic awards. Thus, an individual's ability to list awards and achievements may be more contingent upon where he or she worked rather than what he or she accomplished.

Unusual sizes or colours of paper

Most serious applicants will conform to the norm of A4 paper that is white or off-white in colour. Acceptable alternatives to white include light beige, light gold, and, possibly very light green or very light blue. A CV presented on loud or garishly coloured paper is a strong indication that the applicant is not serious about employment with your company or simply has poor taste. Exceptions include creative positions within advertising or the communications industry or positions in the entertainment field.

The size of the paper used is also important. There's nothing particularly wrong with use of odd size paper, but again, most serious applicants would not take the chance of exhibiting non-conformity in the application process.

Use of company stationery or franking machine

A CV, covering letter or envelope that bears the logo, trademark or insignia of an applicant's current or, perhaps, former company is a dead give-away that this applicant should be disqualified. Use of anyone's stationery but one's own in submitting an application is totally inappropriate and offers a keen indication of the future practices of this person were he or she to be hired by you. The same applies when the current employer's franking machine is used to pay for postage.

Checklist 14

READING BETWEEN THE LINES OF CVs

- ☐ Beware of copies of copies.
- ☐ Reassess the potential of the over-joiner.
- ☐ Be wary of ambiguous dates in employment history.
- ☐ Question the need for an over-long CV.
- ☐ Discount CVs on loud or garishly coloured paper.
- ☐ Disqualify CVs using an employer's stationery or franking machine.

The task of selecting the best person for a position is often difficult, especially in today's job market when any solicitation for applications is likely to result in an avalanche of them. Unfortunately, the fastest way to narrow down the pile is to eliminate those which, for whatever reason, yield information that disqualifies the applicant. It is possible that the CV of a perfectly qualified applicant could contain some of the features cited above. For purposes of efficiency, however, and reliance upon probability, 'reading between the lines' of CVs will help you to get to the final selection faster.

CHAPTER 8

Bringing a New Employee on Board

Once hired and ready to begin work, a new employee's first impression is very important and can often have a strong and lasting effect on the employee's morale. Supplying new employees with all the information they need to feel that they 'belong' is essential. It has been demonstrated that the dividends in good will, morale, and production efficiency greatly outweigh the effort required to make a new employee feel at home.

Many companies have developed a comprehensive orientation procedure. For smaller companies, it is not necessary to establish elaborate procedures; the use of a simple orientation checklist will suffice.

In this chapter we'll review the steps for effectively orienting a new employee to your staff and the organisation. Also, here are some questions that will be answered:

- ☐ What should new employee orientation consist of, at a minimum?
- ☐ Why is it important to structure the time of the new employee?
- ☐ What do orientation checklists contain?
- ☐ What is a probationary period and why is it useful?

Checklist 15

MINIMUM ORIENTATION REQUIREMENTS

- ☐ Introduction to other employees.
- ☐ Tour of facilities.

53

- ☐ Check-in procedures:
  - —Use of clocking-in cards (if applicable)
  - —Issuing of keys, supplies etc.
- ☐ Pay policy: when paid, deductions made.
- ☐ Phoning in procedures.
- ☐ Overview of business operations.
- ☐ Preparation of reports or written materials, and
- ☐ Health insurance forms and any other employee benefit items.

Checklist 16

FOR A MORE COMPLETE ORIENTATION PROGRAMME

Independent of what your organisation may provide in the way of orientation, you should develop your own orientation procedure including:

- ☐ Introduction to colleagues.
- ☐ Taking the employee to a first day lunch.
- ☐ Providing background or project support reading material.

Finally, for a more complete orientation programme you may also consider including the following elements as part of your programme:

- ☐ Organisational history.
- ☐ Discussion of medical and emergency services.
- ☐ Holidays, time off and sick leave.
- ☐ Facilities accessibility after hours and at weekends.
- ☐ Safety procedures and precautions.
- ☐ Promotion and transfer procedures.
- ☐ Grievance procedures.

Some very progressive organisations go to several steps further and send a welcome letter to the new employee's home, issue an introduction card to the new employee to wear for the first week on the job and have one of the top executives welcome the new employee again some time during the first week on the job.

To stimulate some ideas for developing your own system, here is a sample orientation checklist used by a major business machines manufacturer.

Figure 6

Employee orientation procedure

☐ Sales ☐ Systems ☐ Field Engineering ☐ Office

EMPLOYEE'S NAME——————— BRANCH———————

There are many policies and procedures that a new employee is anxious to know and with which he should become acquainted during the first few days of his employment. The following list will assist in covering these points. A tick in the space after each item will suffice to indicate that the item has been discussed with the new employee.

INTRODUCTION — To other members of branch or group—either individually or at meeting, depending upon size of organisation. ☐

BRANCH TOUR — Location of various facilities, telephones, post, parking arrangements, and any other local amenities. ☐

CONFERENCE — With district branch management to obtain an understanding of the respective departments and the relationship to the employee's position. ☐

CONTRACT SUMMARY — Explain key points covered by his contract, including salary and responsibilities. ☐

COVERAGE OF PART 1

SECTION 1.1— ☐
Information regarding the company.

SECTION 1.2— ☐
Employee privileges and benefits. (Give employee booklets on group insurance, retirement plan, union membership etc.)

SECTION 1.3— ☐
Employee responsibilities.

SECTION 1.4— ☐
Employee payroll details, expenses, deductions and loans.

ALSO SUBJECT—
1.4.1-8—Branch hours

FOLLOWING INFORMATION TO BE COVERED WITH ALL EMPLOYEES

A. EMPLOYMENT INFORMATION

———— Standard of conduct

———— Salary administration

———— Discuss performance reviews

———— Explain preparation and use of forms

———— Outline various phases of training programme

———— Reporting of absence or lateness

———— Safety rules

———— Promotional opportunities within company

———— Probationary period

———— Employee suggestions and complaints

B. DEPARTMENTAL INFORMATION

———— 1. Technical library (systems and sales only)
Acquaint with availability and proper use of technical material in library.

———— 2. Set up and explain Form 1391 (sales only)

———— 3. Initiate and explain purpose of Form 1117 (sales only)

———— 4. Advertising and reference material file (sales and systems personnel)

———— 5. Acquaint with qualification requirements for sales school (sales only)

———— 6. Business ethics (sales only)
Review of F.M.M Subject 1.3.11

———— 7. Distribute keys for desks or branch quarters for access to branch after work hours (sales and systems)

———— 8. Dealer programme (field engineering only)
F.M.M. 2.10.15

C. BENEFITS

——— A. Medical coverage
    1. Hospital plan
    2. Surgery
    3. Out-patient

——— B. Major medical coverage

——— C. Claims procedure

——— D. Disability coverage
    1. Service days (where applicable)
    2. Salary continuation
    3. Weekly disability

——— E. Life assurance

——— F. Pension plan
    1. Non-contributory
    2. Contributory

——— G. Educational assistance

——— H. Stock option

——— I. Credit union

——— J. Authorised absences
    1. Holidays
    2. Vacation
    3. Maternity leave
    4. Disability leave
    5. Bereavement leave
    6. Jury duty
    7. Personal leave

ALL EMPLOYEES

I have read and discussed the Company Policies and Procedures as outlined above — In particular the Manual Subject 1.3.1-4 on private dealings has been reviewed and is understood. I will, to the best of my ability, abide by these procedures and policies.

_____   _____

Date   Employer's Signature

In addition to concurring in the above, I have also verified the employee's birthdate to be

_____

month   day   year

from the following source document _____

_____

Date   Signature

_____

Title

A word about probationary periods

Despite thoroughness in the process of selecting new employees, it's wise to base the final decision to retain an employee upon the successful completion of a probationary period. In a sense, both the employee and the company are 'on trial' during the probationary period. Each is evaluating the other and forming impressions which will affect the final decision.

The best time to introduce new employees to the probationary period concept is during the initial interview. However, the nitty gritty explanation and initiation should take place just subsequent to or on the employee's first day. If the trial period is spelled out as part of the customary orientation procedure, then everything generally runs smoothly.

Regardless of its length, a probationary period offers a chance to observe new workers on the job. Regular observations should be made; you should meet with new employees frequently to discuss progress, answer questions, and provide an extra dose of supervision.

When it's time to make a final decision, compare observed performance with the job requirements as reflected in the job descriptions (which, of course, were mutually formulated). If there is any doubt about the employee's ability to do the job, he or she should not be retained. This decision should be arrived at objectively, and discussed tactfully with employees. When unsuitable employees are retained, a disservice is done to them as well as to the department and company as a whole. The mere presence of poor employees can help to cause morale problems for the good employees, and affect the department's and the company's overall efficiency.

Checklist 17

HANDLING PROBATIONARY PERIODS

☐ Introduce the policy early in the interview process.
☐ Institute the policy on the first day.
☐ Meet frequently to help the new employee.
☐ Compare observed performance with job requirements.
☐ Do not retain unsuitable employees.

A word on employee contracts

Written particulars of the terms of employment must be given to all employees not later than 13 weeks from the date they start work. The letter of appointment will contain a basic outline. Mid- and upper-level employees would probably require a contract before joining the organisation. Such employee contracts are useful if you need to protect trade secrets or inventions, and if you need to limit competition from the employee should he or she depart and go into business for himself. The employee contract can also be looked upon as a marketing tool—it assists in attracting top achievers who have well-developed skills in looking out for themselves.

Checklist 18

ELEMENTS OF AN EMPLOYMENT CONTRACT

☐　The written statement of express terms must include:
　　The names of the employer and employee.
　　The date when employment began.
　　A statement whether any employment with a previous employer counts as part of the employee's continuous period of employment, and if so, when it began.
　　Rate of pay.
　　Payment interval.
　　Hours of work.
　　Holiday pay, including entitlement on termination.
　　Sick pay.
　　Pension arrangements.
　　Notice required to terminate employment from both employer and employee.
　　Job title.
　　References must be made to disciplinary rules and procedures and grievance procedures.
☐　The written statement is not the contract itself, but can be taken as an accurate record of it. Also included in contractual documents may be the letter of appointment, staff manuals, works rules and collective agreements which should be mentioned in the letter of appointment.
☐　For higher level staff, an employment contract may additionally incorporate the following items:
　　Fixed period of the contract.
　　Full description of responsibilities.
　　When salary will be reviewed.

Any bonus or commission arrangements.

Long-term incentive awards.

Employee benefits: company cars, insurance, medical insurance, profit sharing and so on.

Arbitration clause.

☐ To minimise problems arising from changes, it may be advisable to avoid too precise a job description in case the work changes, and to include a clause indicating that employees may be required to work at other places.

Part 2

Scheduling for Productivity

Productivity is a difficult concept to define. The term 'productivity' is often bantered about, yet few comprehend its meaning. Industry studies consistently fail to acknowledge the complex effect of multiple inputs and outputs on productivity.

In this book the term 'productivity' will be used to mean systematic efforts to increase, extend, or achieve human and organisational benefit outputs and decrease resource inputs. This definition represents an adaptation of work done by noted productivity expert and author Robert R Carkhuff.

In your role as supervisor you may be required to integrate many elements—human resources, raw materials, supplies, plant and equipment, all within a variety of technical and organisational constraints. The interplay of all of these is usually needed to achieve an end product, but the effective use and supervision of human resources, your staff, is generally your most important responsibility.

Chapters 9 to 14, comprising Part 2, focus on how best to harness natural work patterns and thus schedule the work flow for improved productivity, while sparing you productivity terminology claptrap. This section will be of particular importance to you if you are often unable to account for your staff's periods of low output.

CHAPTER 9

Supervising Cycles of Productivity

Linda won't transcribe tapes late in the day or any time on Friday. In fact, she has established a personal work pattern or cycle in which specific tasks will be undertaken throughout the course of the week.

Susan, the production supervisor, rarely interferes with Linda's cycle unless an urgent report or letter must be completed. Is Linda an obstinate employee, undermining production needs of her office? Is Susan deficient as a production supervisor? For the surprising answer to these questions plus the ones below, turn the page.

☐ What is a personal cycle of productivity?
☐ How can the supervisor best take advantage of good employees' cycles?
☐ What benefits accrue to acknowledging good employees' cycles?
☐ What are ways to get the most out of productive employees?
☐ How does an office crisis affect an employee's cycle?
☐ Do supervisors have cycles of productivity?

Recognising the cycle

Returning to the scenario of Susan and Linda, is either woman derelict in her duties?

For either woman, quite the contrary. Linda is an exceptionally effective member of the production staff, and Susan directs the production department skilfully. Linda has long determined her productive peaks and troughs throughout the course of the normal work week, and hence recognises her personal cycle of productivity. For all but urgent assignments, Susan acknowledges Linda's ability to maintain high productivity by handling assignments on those days and at those hours which achieve a relatively constant 'effort to task' ratio.

Roberta, Linda's equally efficient production staff partner, also maintains high productivity by personally prioritising assignments. While Linda and Roberta have similar production responsibilities, each has different strengths and weaknesses, varying energy levels (throughout the working week), and has long since gauged these factors so that each knows what can best be undertaken when.

Employees establish their cycles

Good employees should be afforded the opportunity to establish their personal productivity cycles and, within reason, should be allowed to undertake assignments in a manner which best suits them. So many employees devise countless ways to diminish personal productivity by stretching out assignments, or by coasting until it's time to go. However, highly productive employees such as Linda, Roberta and Susan take pride in consistently maintaining high productivity. Enabling them to respond in phase with personal cycles of productivity results in high job satisfaction and yields a greater long-range output.

Another reason to let productive people follow their own schedules is that they will be less fatigued. It is quite draining to be continually meeting often arbitrary deadlines or to undertake selective tasks when one does not feel fully equipped to do so. Productive employees, allowed to pace themselves, can accomplish more and remain more vibrant.

How to get the most out of productive employees

Productive employees may have an internal 'time grid' that charts their cycle of productivity. Quite often, no formal sketch or chart is ever made. Nevertheless, it does exist. Productive employees may also be reluctant to tell supervisors that they'd 'rather not handle the DEF report right now' because they 'can do a better job on it tomorrow morning' and the 'GHI assignment could be better undertaken now'.

Apart from discussion, there are four basic ways to get the most from productive employees taking cycles of productivity into account.

1. Provide enough and varied assignments so the cycle can be used. If an employee has only one assignment then obviously there is little leeway in undertaking the assignment at the most personally opportune time. With numerous assignments, a productive employee can strategically arrange his or her schedule.
2. Be flexible over 'due' dates when possible. Productive employees will finish the important jobs on time. Assignments of lesser importance will be finished as soon as possible. The more flexibility a productive employee is given in completing assignments, the greater the opportunity for him or her to execute assignments in accordance with the cycle. More often than not, given flexible due dates, the productive employee will complete many assignments sooner than you anticipated.

3. Avoid late afternoon and surprise assignments. The productive employee, in concurrence with his or her cycle of productivity, intuitively allocates tasks for the late afternoon. (For an extended view of the harm in issuing late afternoon assignments, see Chapter 25.)
4. Closely related to the above, always try to provide advance notice of assignments to productive employees so that sufficient time is available to schedule the new assignment in accordance with the cycle of productivity. If you usually provide flexible due dates, then the need for advanced notice is not essential.

Reprogramming the cycle

A good worker's cycle of productivity can be reprogrammed to meet the needs of the organisation, company or department. For example, if an important report must be finished within four days, good employees will prepare themselves and will generate the requisite energy to accomplish the task successfully. In the short run, good employees can reprogramme their cycles of productivity to handle a crisis.

However, forcing a good worker to reprogramme his or her cycle for an extended period is not recommended. Since he or she is already highly efficient, an extended variation soon becomes an imposition, and can upset the delicate balance by which the productive employee remains productive.

Supervisors and managers have cycles of productivity too. After all, you chose to read this chapter at *this* particular time, didn't you?

Checklist 19

SUPERVISING CYCLES OF PRODUCTIVITY

☐ Let good employees establish and follow their cycles.
☐ Provide enough assignments so the cycle can be effectively used.
☐ Be flexible as to due dates (when possible).
☐ Avoid late afternoon and surprise assignments.
☐ Give advance notice of assignments (when possible).
☐ Avoid forcing reprogramming of a cycle for an extended period.
☐ Recognise your own cycle and work with it!

In the next chapter we'll discuss how the effective supervisor streamlines his or her own schedule.

CHAPTER 10
Streamlining Your Act

In order to supervise others effectively and schedule their tasks and activities, it's necessary first to be able to schedule effectively your own tasks and activities. Streamlining your act means being able to set goals and maintain personal time management.

The supervisor who's always changing course, or chasing the clock, will have a difficult time effectively scheduling the staff. By 'streamlining your act' you establish a model which employees may emulate, and increase the quality of the time that you put into the job.

This chapter will help you to answer the following questions:

- [ ] When goal setting, why is it useful to exceed the number of the goals you'd like to accomplish?
- [ ] What is meant by ready, fire, aim?
- [ ] How does establishing files in advance enhance personal time management?
- [ ] What is meant by multiple stations?
- [ ] What are some techniques for 'creating' time?
- [ ] What is the single greatest time saver?

The magic of goal setting

In 1954, the graduating class of Yale University was polled to determine what percentage of the class had established written financial goals. Some 86 per cent of the class had established no goals whatsoever, while 11 per cent had established some goals but had either not written them down or could not produce them if requested, and only 3 per cent had clearly established well-defined, written financial goals.

In 1974, a follow-up study was done on Yale's 1954 graduating class. To the amazement of those conducting the study, the 3 per cent who in 1954 had clearly established well-defined written goals, now had a combined net worth that exceeded the other 97 per cent of the graduating class combined! Undoubtedly, you have read or heard of the importance of setting goals. While we all maintain some notion of where we wish to head, the goal-setting process is often shortchanged.

Checklist 20
GOAL SETTING TIPS

- ☐ Over select. When choosing goals that you wish to accomplish as a supervisor on the job and for your own career, initially, over select. After listing all of the things you'd like to accomplish go back and realistically assess those that are top priority versus those that are nice but, on second inspection, not that important.
- ☐ Remember 'Less is more'. A few well-chosen goals that are challenging, yet reachable are preferable when making your selection. It is of no value to anyone to choose unrealistic, unreachable goals that lead only to frustration and despair.
- ☐ Reduce 'interruptions' or 'noise'. Once you've chosen challenging, but reachable goals, tune out all other distractions. You reach a goal that much sooner and are better prepared to establish new goals as time and resources permit.
- ☐ Publicise your goals. Many successful supervisors and managers have had their goals typed up, then reduced and laminated, or photocopied and distributed for convenient and frequent review. The easiest way to stay on target is to review periodically the goals you've established, daily if necessary, so as to remain in a highly focused, on-target mode. When you and your staff are operating in such a manner, great results can be accomplished.
- ☐ Build in flexibility. While it's important to establish a few well-chosen goals, recognise that the nature of your responsibilities and tasks often changes and a goal that was necessary and appropriate yesterday may suddenly no longer be valid. While remaining steadfast and on-target in pursuit of your goals, also assess them objectively to determine their present and continuing applicability. The ability to change or shift with your organisation's or department's needs is as important as your ability to select appropriate goals.

Ready, fire, aim

Peters and Waterman, authors of *In Search of Excellence*, observed that for too many years American businesses were stuck in the 'ready, aim, fire' mode—in order to get ready to undertake a project, reams of study, analysis, assessment and evaluation were first undertaken, followed by careful planning, test marketing, or simulation and then firing—finally diving headlong into the project or market area.

The 'ready, fire, aim' concept which can readily be used at a project level involves making a brief evaluation or assessment of the task at hand, followed by an early 'firing' involving getting into the actual project activity even if on a piecemeal or limited basis, and then 'aiming' which involves readjusting, modifying or honing project plans. The 'ready, fire, aim' concept is useful and important to supervisors because it effectively shortens the time in which full-scale project activities can be initiated while minimising the risk of misfiring or misallocating resources. If you are operating on a limited budget (and who isn't?) then the 'ready, fire, aim' concept may well be a necessity.

Establishing milestones

Establishing milestones for the realisation or completion of the goals you've chosen is essential for successful supervision. Normally the period that you have to accomplish goals is implicit in the situation—deadlines have been imposed from above or from the market-place.

Preparing a milestone chart is an easy way to maintain command of the timing and progress toward established goals. A simple milestone chart, such as that presented on the following page can be prepared, which delineates each task and subtask including starting time, ending time and a schedule of delivery of products. There are numerous software applications that can be used in preparing milestone charts.

The calendar block back method assures that a goal will be achieved and milestones reached by using the monthly calendar. Here's how it works. Start from the due date or deadline for which a task, project or delivery must be completed. Then plot the subtasks and activities that must be undertaken from that due date to the present day. In other words, work backwards using the monthly calendar to establish realistic, interim dates that reflect organisational resources, staff vacation time, holidays, weekends and other down-time and which reflect reasonable output levels.

By using the calendar block back method, you can quickly determine that if, for example, subtask two in pursuit of goal X was accomplished two days late, then the whole project will be two days late unless immediate corrective action is taken.

One exceptionally effective supervisor used to schedule projects to be finished a full week before the actual deadline by treating the artificial deadline as real. In this way the supervisor always finished projects on time or early.

It has been suggested that a reasonable scheduling rule of thumb is to estimate how much time you think a given activity or task will take and multiply it by 1.25. If the task is something that's never been undertaken before, multiply the time you think it will take by 1.5. A common weakness among capable people is that they sometimes unrealistically estimate the time it will take to accomplish something. By adding a small safety margin, the probability of assembling the requisite resources and finishing the project on time increases.

Figure 7

Milestone chart for timetabling

SUBTASK	AUG.	SEPT.	OCT.	NOV.
PREPARE BIBLIOGRAPHY				
A. Compile list				
B. Analyse list				
C. Prepare list				
D. Prepare camera-ready				
E. Submit				△27
PREPARE SUPPLEMENTARY MATERIAL				
A. Determine need				
B. Make rec.		△28		
C. Draft copy				
D. Develop graphics				
E. Prepare camera-ready				
F. Submit				△29
PREPARE RECOMMENDATIONS				
A. Determine need				
B. Prepare report				
C. Submit				△30

MILESTONE KEY

Milestone	Project Date	Comment	Actual Completion Date
27. Submit Bibliography	29/10		
28. Make Rec.	21/9		
29. Submit Sup.	29/10		
30. Submit Recs.	8/11		

Figure 8
Calendar block back

MONTH __March__   YEAR __19XX__

Sunday	Monday	Tuesday	Wednesday	Thursday	Friday	Saturday
	1 Submitted Feb 24	2 Deliver draft workshop planning report	3	4	5	6
7	8	9 Submitted to typing	10	11	12	13
14	15 Assessment of conf capabilities Deliver profile revisions	16	17	18	19 Assessment of target audience, 52 pages. Deliver	20
21	22	23	24	25	26	27
28	29	30 Deliver final workshop planning report	31			

Insiders' tips

Here are some other suggestions, which I have found to work very well, for augmenting your personal schedule. First, recognise that establishing files in advance, taking the time to get organised, and assembling the necessary resources to undertake a project may not seem like whirl-wind activities, yet greatly contribute to your overall project effort.

Another technique is the use of multiple stations. An example will illustrate. If you wear contact lenses, you know that it makes sense to keep extra solution and lens containers in your desk at work, at home, in your car and in your locker at the gym. In this way you're always prepared without having to carry these materials on your person.

So it is with supervision.

The resources you may choose to post at multiple stations may include pens, note pads, calculators etc. If you use these items enough and the need may occur at any of several locations, free yourself from having to carry them by setting up stations in advance.

As any good supervisor knows, one of the best ways to save time is to delegate. Even better is to not do a task—by that I mean any task or activity that can safely be eliminated, should be eliminated.

You can also 'create' time by imagining you've been assigned to undertake a project on your own say, every Tuesday morning from 9 to 11. The project is to run 15 weeks and you must do it alone, undisturbed. Now that you've cleared away the next 15 Tuesdays from 9 to 11 in the morning, sit back and relax since there really is no project of this nature assigned to you. However, with this mental framework and some self-discipline you can maintain two free hours every Tuesday morning for a 15-week period.

Checklist 21

STREAMLINING YOUR ACT

- ☐ Remember the magic of goal setting, and set your goals now.
- ☐ Over select the goals you wish to accomplish, prioritise them and start on the important ones.
- ☐ Eliminate distractions, interruptions, noise!
- ☐ Publicise your goals.
- ☐ Build flexibility into your schedule.
- ☐ Use the ready, fire, aim method.
- ☐ Establish milestones and a milestone chart.

- ☐ Use calendar block back to ensure that deadlines will be met.
- ☐ Multiply how much time you think a task will take by 1.25.
- ☐ Establish files and get organised in advance.
- ☐ Use multiple stations so that you can carry less.
- ☐ Delegate.
- ☐ Eliminate what can be eliminated.
- ☐ Create time by assuming an imaginary assignment.

Now let's take a look at some of the ways your staff engage in non-productive activity—favourite employee time-wasters.

CHAPTER 11

Favourite Employee Time-wasters

In addition to serving in the role for which they are employed, employees engage in other activities during business hours. On the pages that follow is a review of favourite employee time-wasters: those events, practices and phenomena that infringe upon the output and effectiveness of an organisation, company, department or division. While isolated incidences may not in themselves have a sizeable effect on overall company performance, repetitive occurrence by numerous employees will indeed have a pronounced effect.

It's not likely that any of the time wasters to be discussed will be news to you. At one time or another you've probably engaged in a few of them yourself. From the perspective of management and supervision, however, it will be useful to examine employees' favourite time wasting activities anew.

This chapter provides the answers to these questions:

- [ ] How costly can 'coasting' until check-out time be?
- [ ] Can one be over-organised?
- [ ] How can employees take two lunch breaks on the same day?
- [ ] Is waiting for pay packets a time-waster?
- [ ] Why must time sheets be filled in on a continuing basis rather than once per week?
- [ ] What are five ways the 'plastered' employee causes harm?

Coasting until check-out time

Many employees at the end of their working day, have a tendency to stop work 15 to 30 minutes in advance and coast until leaving.

While it is not possible for everyone to remain productive during the closing minutes of each day, if the phenomenon of coasting until closing time is widespread within a department, or throughout an entire company, the net loss can be staggering.

As an illustration, if 45 employees out of a total of 450, habitually coast for the last 30 minutes of each day, and if the average wage is £5 per hour, during one month containing 20 working days, the company will page £2250 for non-productive time. Adding benefits and other costs incurred yields a figure of over £2800. On a yearly basis their figure rises to over £33 000

45 employees × £5.00/hr × 30 minutes/day × 20 days = £2250
£2250/month × 1.25 (for benefits) × 12 months = £33,750.

If the time spent 'coasting' is used to plan the next working day or to make mental preparations for future tasks, then this time use becomes productive. However, if many employees use their last 15 or 30 minutes of each day to merely watch the clock and wait until its hands finally reach their departure hour, then a major problem exists.

Clock watching may also occur prior to the lunch hour. Many employees coast for 15 to 20 minutes before lunch, as well as prior to coffee breaks, department meetings and other planned events.

Organisation and reorganisations

Another favourite time-waster is the continual organisation and reorganisation of desks, files, shelves etc. One's working materials can only be organised so many times before a state of diminishing return is reached, after which time there is no advantage in continuing. As a general rule, if someone is able to extract needed information from desks or files within a minute or two, then he or she is sufficiently organised. Any further time invested in the organisation or reorganisation of materials is a waste of time.

Secretaries and clerical workers often avoid typing or other tasks in favour of activities that they perceive as being easier or less tedious, such as filing or labelling. Those employees that use the last 15 to 30 minutes of the day to organise themselves for the next day, so that they may start fresh on new projects or resume with renewed vigour are, however, making good use of time. (See Chapter 12.)

Moreover, it is recommended that employees take a few minutes at the end of each day and each week to prepare for the coming day or week. Thus, it is possible that an employee may appear to be 'coasting' until closing time, or to be organising or over organising, while they are actually engaging in a useful and productive period.

Carefully reading junk mail

The mail order houses, national manufacturers and distributors, and business and professional services groups all use the post to build business. Any employee who has been with an organisation for longer than three months is bound to receive a steady stream of junk mail as his or her name is added to an ever growing number of mailing lists. An employee may receive five to ten pieces of unsolicited mail per day. When this occurs, it is important for the employee to judge accurately what should be read and acted upon, what should be filed for future use, and what should be discarded immediately. Unfortunately, many employees take delight in reading every piece of information that has been sent to them and use the reviewing of mail as a procrastination technique.

It is nearly impossible to legislate how mail should be circulated to employees. Holding the mail until late in the day is not recommended because an employee may need a vital piece of information.

Taking two lunch breaks

This technique has been widely practised particularly in job shop and factory settings where an employee may easily sneak behind machinery or other shelter and munch his or her sandwich prior to the designated lunch hour. When the designated lunch hour arrives, the employee has created 'time' beyond that previously taken while eating lunch.

This practice is unfair to the company. In a factory setting, it is potentially dangerous. Within an office setting, spills and food stains often end up on company documents and paper work which diminishes the professionalism of the entire office. Unless there is a designated area within your organisation where an employee may have refreshment, and other than during designated coffee or meal breaks, employees should be discouraged from consuming food at work stations.

Related to eating lunch before the designated time is the practice of employees bringing breakfast to work. It is often difficult for an employee to eat breakfast before departing for work, particularly in an urban setting where one has to fight morning traffic. However, allowing employees to bring breakfast into work produces harmful side effects:

Checklist 22

HARMFUL EFFECTS OF BREAKFAST AT WORK

☐ The amount of time that the employee spends eating breakfast is, of course, non-productive time to the company;

☐ Those employees that have adequately planned their day and ate breakfast before departing for work are, in essence, penalised;

☐ The potential for soiling papers or other company owned equipment is high; and

☐ The practice detracts from the professionalism of the entire organisation.

Waiting for pay slips

An all-time favourite employee time-waster is waiting for the pay slip. Whether pay slips are delivered on Fridays, bi-weekly or monthly, most employees are keenly aware of pay day. If the time of the day at which the pay slip arrives varies, many employees will shuffle through the day waiting until the check actually arrives and then make a mad dash to the bank for a deposit. Others may be anxious about the slip not coming or containing an incorrect total.

The best policy in fighting this time waster is to distribute the slips at the same time each pay day. Thus, it will be known throughout the company that slips will be delivered exactly at 11.30 am, and employees can plan accordingly. It might be wise to issue slips immediately on pay day so that employees may receive their slips, take care of personal responsibilities, and get back to work. Distributing pay slips early in the day also has the advantage of reducing the time that employees waste precalculating the figures that the slips should contain or being anxious as to what the amount will be.

Excessive, elaborate travel arrangements

Often when an employee has to travel, he or she has the tendency to spend more time on travel plans than is necessary. For example, when an employee has to travel for business reasons, particularly to an area that is near resort facilities, there is a tendency for additional time to be wasted beyond that of normal pre-trip banter, discussing the trip.

One way to eliminate time frittered away on travel plans is to have a clerical or support person to complete all travel arrangements including the itinerary, and submit a comprehensive travel package to the employee who has been authorised to travel. At the very least, this will eliminate some of the questions and conjecture as to where one will stay, when one will be arriving, and so forth.

Extensive review of time sheets

In nearly all organisations some type of time sheet or weekly reporting log must be completed and submitted to management. If this time sheet or log has been compiled on a daily basis, when Friday or the end of the recording period rolls around, there will be relatively little to do to complete the form.

However, if an employee does not enter the required data on a daily, or at least regular basis, at the end of the reporting period an extensive compilation and review of the time sheet or log will be necessary. The fact is that the time expended in trying to complete a time sheet a week later is far in excess of the time required to record information daily. Thus, employees should be instructed to maintain time sheets or logs on a daily or regular basis.

Getting plastered on Friday afternoons

A large number of employees, particularly in city office environments, think nothing of getting plastered in a local pub on a Friday during the lunch hour. (Note: some prefer to get stoned.) Often, what should have been 60 minutes or less turns into two hours and more, and the employee's productivity for the rest of the day is virtually nil. What's worse, some decide to 'celebrate' the end of the week as early as

Thursday afternoon, and use the Thursday lunch period, as well as Friday, to get plastered.

This favourite employee time-waster can only continue to flourish in the absence of good supervision. While it is common to conduct a farewell lunch for a departing employee, have a holiday celebration, or hold a staff luncheon following a good monthly or quarterly effort, if a sufficient number of employees get plastered every other Friday, significant costs to the company are incurred. Other liabilities to the company that accrue when employees get plastered on Friday include the following:

Checklist 23

LIABILITIES OF EMPLOYEES WHO DRINK TOO MUCH

☐ The productivity of the employee is low;
☐ The employee's judgement and decision-making capabilities are diminished;
☐ The employee may not be able to represent the company adequately with on-site visitors or over the telephone;
☐ The hard-working, non-imbibing employee may be resentful; and
☐ The professionalism of the organisation has been diminished.

There are many other time-wasters. The supervisor who is at least aware of some traditional time-wasters will more readily be able to acknowledge when they are occurring, and be able to diminish their effect.

Checklist 24

EMPLOYEE TIME-WASTERS

Here's a checklist of favourite employee time wasters. Read it to your staff and convey the message that all such practices are to be eliminated:

☐ Coasting until checkout time
☐ Over organising

- ☐ Reading junk mail carefully
- ☐ Taking two lunch breaks
- ☐ Waiting for pay slips
- ☐ Making excessive travel plans
- ☐ Completing time sheets once per week
- ☐ Getting plastered at lunch

In Chapter 12 we'll explore effective ways to combat some of the time-wasters.

CHAPTER 12
Using Friday Afternoons Profitably

Late one Friday afternoon Bill Halloran walked past several offices of employees whom he supervised and noticed that about half didn't seem to be working. Many were on the telephone conducting casual conversations, apparently with friends or spouses; others were milling about, idly chattering or absorbed in some minor activity.

This didn't upset Bill because he realized that as the weekend approached it seemed nearly impossible for any supervisor to maintain a staff of fully alert and productive employees. Moreover, it is human nature to dwell upon that which we will be doing once the working day or working week has ended.

In this chapter we'll explore what can be done during seemingly 'low productivity periods' and answer the questions:

- [ ] How can Bill's own attitude affect operations?
- [ ] Is filing a worthwhile activity late in the day?
- [ ] Is it all right for Bill to meet the staff for a drink after work?
- [ ] How can Bill better prepare staff for the following week?
- [ ] What does an open door policy encourage?

Several weeks passed and Bill, an excellent supervisor, wondered if there weren't some ways to increase productivity on Friday afternoons while not appearing authoritarian or causing resentment and demoralizing his staff. After a while, Bill concluded that there were ways to accomplish his goal and that the best method for achieving the desired results was to develop a low-key, informal strategy to guide the staff favourably.

File, file, file

First, Bill individually suggested to several employees that late Friday afternoon was a good time to make sure that personal and common files were in order, purged of unnecessary documents and properly catalogued or indexed. Bill's company was generally interested in reducing paper handling, and Friday afternoon was a particularly good time to reduce paper files when the material was available on disc or other data processing medium.

Bill also suggested that insurance and medical forms and miscellaneous correspondence be handled on Friday afternoons. The rationale for this suggestion is clear—filling in forms is largely routine work which does not require heavy thinking and thus is a suitable activity during the time in which employees are most distracted.

The open door

Without telling anyone, but making it rather obvious, Bill made available the last two hours of his Friday to any of his staff that wished to speak to him. Bill found that as the week drew to a close his staff were much more likely to open up and discuss problems or, perhaps, offer new suggestions to improve operations.

As the weeks went by, Bill was often able to speak to as many as three or four of his staff, individually, late on Friday. Bill also encouraged project supervisors to meet informally with team members so that everyone could be up and running next Monday morning.

An occasional social hour

Now and then somebody in Bill's staff decided to get a group together after work to enjoy the Happy Hour at a nearby bar. Bill was frequently asked if he would attend such occasions and usually said yes. He did this for two reasons: one, he genuinely liked his staff and liked to socialise with them for an hour or so on occasion after work; and two, he recognised that staff morale and productivity was generally higher on those Fridays in which it was known staff members would be meeting after work for a drink. Thus Bill supported this social venture, left his title back in the office, and became one of the gang.

Mixing lower and higher priority tasks

Bill recognised that initiating new tasks late in the afternoon, particularly on Friday afternoon, was never well received and generally represented bad policy. However, he did hit upon the idea of occassionally requesting selected staff members to undertake a small task which would later support a more important project. For example, he asked Mark Flumen to outline the steps that would be necessary to solve a particular company problem.

The outline needed to be only one or two pages. Mark did a good job on this seemingly lower priority task. Next Monday Bill assigned to Mark the writing of a formal report based on the outline and asked him to lead a team which would implement the suggestions and recommendations made. In asking Mark to prepare the outline Bill neither requested a deadline nor formally assigned the task to Mark. Bill was merely seeking some good ideas for solving the problem and had a hunch that Mark could be productively engaged even late on Friday afternoon.

Attitude adjustment

Finally, and perhaps most importantly, Bill realised that his own attitude regarding productivity late on Friday afternoon and the manner in which he pursued his tasks during this period would heavily influence his staff. Bill knew of other supervisors who had largely given in to the 'Thank God it's Friday' syndrome as early as 3 pm. He resolved that it was necessary not to let down his guard and exhibit *de facto* acceptance of slacking off towards the weekend. In this way Bill was able to influence his employees to maintain a solid work effort most effectively.

Here's a checklist for future reference:

Checklist 25

USING LATE AFTERNOONS PROFITABLY

- ☐ Use a low key informal strategy.
- ☐ Encourage employees to file materials or complete miscellaneous forms and correspondence.
- ☐ Initiate an open door policy.
- ☐ Join the staff for an occasional social hour.
- ☐ Initiate future tasks as a creative exercise.

☐ Plan next week's schedule.
☐ Maintain your proper attitude: lead by example.

Is there a way to let your staff work flexible hours while not disrupting your scheduling? Yes. Chapter 13 explores alternative work schedules.

CHAPTER 13

Exploring Alternative Work Schedules

The communications and computer revolution, combined with the emerging role of women in the workforce and the varied and dynamic nature of the nuclear family, requires supervisors that can ably direct employees requiring a flexible work schedule. The old formula of nine-to-five with two weeks' summer holiday is rapidly giving way to a host of alternative work patterns designed to meet the individual needs of the employees while maintaining the same level of productivity and efficiency for the organisation.

This chapter focuses on some of the more popular alternative work schedules or flexitime schedules, examines other possible variations in work schedules and will help you to answer these questions:

☐ What are the various flexitime schedules that can be implemented?
☐ Which schedules may fit the needs of your staff?

Eight hours flexitime, with core time

Under this plan, employees may come to work at any time between, say, 7 am and 9.30 am, and depart eight hours later taking into account company policy on time allocated for lunch. Core time refers to those hours in which employees *must* be on site or at the assigned work station. Often core time will be from 10 am to 12 noon, from 1.30 to 3.30 pm or a long period such as 9 am to 3 pm. An established core time affords the supervisor the ability to schedule meetings with staff who may be otherwise arriving and departing at varying times.

Variable day

This plan is much like that above except the number of hours worked per day may vary as long as core time is maintained and the total hours per week add up to 40 (or the assigned number). Some employers set a maximum of 10 hours per day.

Figure 9

Eight hours flexitime, with core time

Flexible time	Core time	Flexible time
7.00 am	9.00 am 3.00 pm	5.00 pm

Figure 10

Variable day

	6.00 am		10		2		6.00 pm
M							10
T			**Core Time**				7
W			**(Includes ½-hour lunch)**				10
Th							8
F							5

Total hours worked weekly = 40

Four 10-hour days

A popular plan with employees is to work four 10-hour days, four days a week with one weekday off per week. This weekday is usually fixed, which affords supervisors and managers ease and ability to schedule meetings, use equipment and allocate other organisational resources.

One potential drawback to this plan is that many employees cannot effectively maintain productivity for the duration of the working day, thus the supervisor effectively gains only eight hours of productive output from the employee for the equivalent of four days while the organisation pays them for the equivalent of five days. For those employees that can maintain productivity however, this plan can be mutually beneficial.

Figure 11

Four-day week

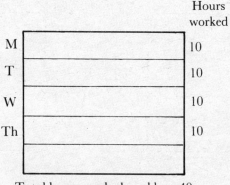

Total hours worked weekly = 40

Nine-hour days, alternating four and five day working weeks

With this plan employees are afforded the opportunity to work nine-hour days for five days of working week number one, and nine-hours days for four days of working week number two. Thus, an employee on this plan will work a total of 81 hours over nine days. Usually the second Friday of the two-week period is the day that is taken off, although this may vary subject to individual working arrangements.

Good employees who tend to come in a little early and to leave a little late may like this plan as it rewards them with 26 more days off per year while only requiring a slightly longer day than they would have put in anyway. From the company's standpoint this is a sound plan because there's less likelihood of the fatigue or low productivity factor with the nine-hour day than the ten-hour.

Figure 12

5—4/9

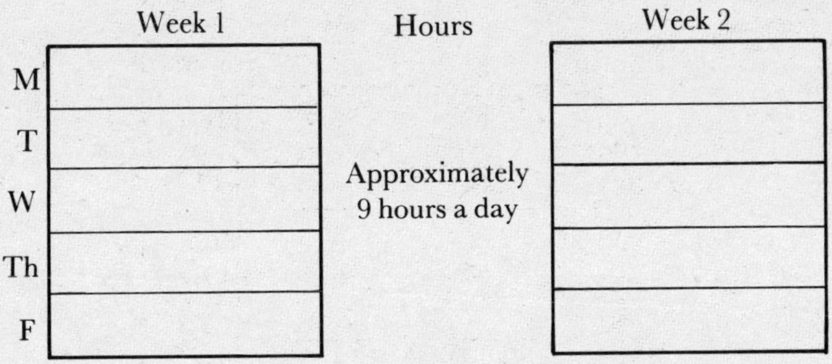

	Week 1	Hours	Week 2
M			
T		Approximately	
W		9 hours a day	
Th			
F			

10-9-8-7-6

Under this plan employees put in long days at the beginning of the week often starting with ten hours on Monday, decreasing the number of hours by one Tuesday to Friday. This plan affords supervisor and employees the ability to get into high gear early in the week while being able to leave progressively earlier each day towards the weekend. This work schedule is advantageous for employees who are better workers at the beginning of the week or find it difficult to maintain the same pace by the fourth or fifth working day.

Figure 13

10-9-8-7-6

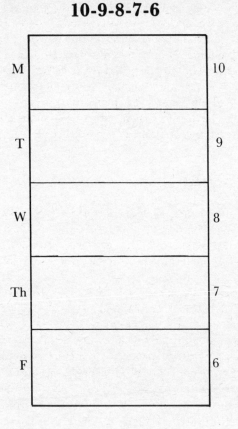

M	10
T	9
W	8
Th	7
F	6

On-site, off-site

With the growing sophistication of remote terminals, personal computers and other online devices, an increasing number of employees can effectively execute tasks and responsibilities at home or from other off-site work places. Under this arrangement the supervisor stays in touch with the employee by telephone, electronic message or other device during those days the employee is off-site. On-site responsibilities, reporting, and meetings are scheduled to ensure that productivity and effectiveness are maintained; supervisor and employee can have first-hand contact and feedback with one another; and the employee gains the necessary social interaction and feeling of team or corporate spirit that may be vital for morale and company loyalty.

The six-day working week

Depending on your type of operation and the company's location the six-day working week may be advantageous for some. Under this plan employees or staff come in to work six days per week generally for six hours and 40 minutes Monday to Saturday. Productivity studies have shown that this plan can be extremely effective because employees working under seven hours per day can maintain a high degree of productivity and efficiency. This plan is particularly useful for those pursuing advanced degrees or some other programme of study, or those who, for whatever reason, prefer to depart early each day.

Looking ahead

In the years ahead changes in the work place may accelerate even more. Modular office components, increasing use of temporary and subcontracted services, voice recognition technology and a host of emerging developments all but ensure that the work place of the late 80s may well undergo a profound change.

Already some data and word processing centres, research and development laboratories, maintenance and repair, and other organisational units are employed around the clock to optimise investment in plant and equipment or other resources.

For a few employees, particularly those involved in physical activity for at least some portion of the working day, three-day working weeks of 13 hours and two minutes (every other day) may be possible. For others, work scheduling may consist of a creative approach based on a 16-hour day or 168-hour working month.

Today's effective supervisor must be prepared to meet the challenge of what Alvin Toffler calls 'third-wave society', wherein the very notion of the traditional working week, for many, may soon disappear. Moreover, companies and organisations that do not meet the varied needs of employees through flexible or alternative work schedules may find their ability to compete for labour resources hampered.

Here's a quick run down on the flexitime programmes discussed in this chapter:

Checklist 26

FLEXITIME PROGRAMMES

☐ *Eight hours flexitime, with core time* — eight-hour days, variable arrival and departure times while maintaining presence during core time.

☐ *Variable day* — total hours worked equals 40, the employee has the option of varying the length of each working day while maintaining presence for a pre-established core time, and the maximum time per day that may be credited to the total working week is approximately 10 hours.

☐ *Four-day week* — most commonly involves four consecutive 10-hour working days.

☐ *5-4/9* — employee works five consecutive days, approximately nine hours a day. During the following working week, employee works four consecutive days, approximately nine hours a day. Pattern of weeks one and two is repeated thereafter.

☐ *10-9-8-7-6* — good for those who work best early in the week.

☐ *On-site, off-site* — increasing occurrence with emergence of personal computer technology.

☐ *Six day working week* — six days of six hours and forty minutes yields high productivity; useful for evening students.

Now, what factors lead to and stimulate creativity and give an added dimension to your performance? Turn to Chapter 14.

Nurturing Your Creativity

Eric Lowe supervised a staff of eight in the credit and finance division of a large department store chain. He noticed that when the temperature in his office was a bit on the high side he wasn't able to think as clearly as he'd like to. Eric also felt quite certain that he did his best creative thinking very early in the morning before everyone else came in and that this was facilitated by a good cup of coffee. Often he sat in the upholstered chair in his office but concluded that, while it was comfortable, he really didn't get much accomplished when sitting there.

If you've ever wondered what factors help to nurture your creativity, this is your chapter. In it look for the answers to the following questions:

☐ What factors lead to errors and unproductive activity?
☐ What kind of weather do most people find aids their creative thinking process?
☐ How can you determine what time of day is best for you to undertake a creative challenge?
☐ What other factors stimulate or hinder the creative thought process?

Control your environment

Many supervisors, just like Eric, start the day with a burst of energy hoping for a flash of inspiration and a little time to themselves to think. While it's not always possible to control your work environment just as you'd like to, there are many elements that should be addressed immediately. Poor lighting or poor ventilation would cramp anyone's style. One renowned speaker and management consultant Dave Yoho, president of Dave Yoho and Associates in Fairfax, Virginia, uses full spectrum lighting so that his employees will be more alert and energetic each day.

Excessive noise, too little working room or extreme temperatures will hamper your creative capabilities.

What's the weather?

Do you realise that most people do some of their best creative thinking when it is raining, snowing, overcast or stormy? The reasons for this aren't exactly clear, but perhaps a nice day filled with bright sunshine is a foil to the creative thinking process. If you're one of those people who does think creatively when the weather outside is frightful, why not 'go with the flow'. Look over that long-term plan that's been sitting in your upper drawer for several weeks past. Or schedule your staff for a brainstorming session (Chapter 18) to overcome current problems.

What time is it?

NASA consultant Paul Blanchard likes to rise at about 10 or 11 am and retire at 2 am to capture 'the best times of the day'. Most individuals find that their period of highest creativity is early in the morning while a significant number find that their peak period is mid-morning or late at night. A far lesser number find their most creative time in the evening and less than one in 12 people judge themselves to be creative during the afternoon.

If you're not sure what time of day you are at your creative best, monitor yourself over one or two weeks. This can be done by keeping a time log of what activities you undertake and when, and also by noting your energy level and enthusiasm throughout the various parts of each day. (Note: see also Chapter 9, Supervising Cycles of Productivity.)

As a result of keeping this log you may be surprised to find that you should perhaps schedule meetings, write reports, or undertake professional reading on a different schedule than hitherto.

Maybe these help creativity

Other factors that may be conducive to your personal creativity include, but are not limited to:

Checklist 27

FACTORS CONDUCIVE TO PERSONAL PRODUCTIVITY

- ☐ Comfortable clothes.
- ☐ Extra space on your desk (a desk is not a filing cabinet!).
- ☐ Your favourite writing instrument.
- ☐ Changing your physical posture (for example, walking, pacing, standing).
- ☐ Readjusting the height of your seat.
- ☐ Altering the firmness or softness of your seat.
- ☐ Experimenting with the type, size, and colour of paper used to write on.

These could hinder creativity

While there's no hard evidence, it's quite possible that these factors could hinder your creative thought process and thus should at least be considered:

Checklist 28

FACTORS THAT HINDER CREATIVE THOUGHT

- ☐ Your phone ringing.
- ☐ The colour of your office walls.
- ☐ The presence or absence of background sounds.
- ☐ The feeling of impending interruptions.
- ☐ The anticipation that just sitting and thinking does not look productive.
- ☐ Too little sleep.
- ☐ Too much sleep.
- ☐ Heavy breads, pasta, or meats for lunch; also a high fat meal.
- ☐ Missing breakfast.
- ☐ Scheduling too tightly.
- ☐ Fear of criticism.

Look around your office and the offices that surround you. Are there factors that you can identify that inhibit your creativity? If so, determine if you can effectively remove or diminish them.

Worth fighting for

If you're like most managers or supervisors you've undoubtedly experienced days and weeks on end when you hardly had a moment to think, let alone a moment to undertake highly creative thinking. This is a serious mistake and one that should not continue to be given 'back burner' status. As supervisor, your ability to schedule yourself and your staff effectively for greatest output depends upon your ability to nurture your creativity.

Checklist 29
TIPS FOR NURTURING CREATIVITY

☐ Control your environment—eliminate poor lighting, poor ventilation, excessive noise, too little working room or extreme temperatures.
☐ Determine your creative hours.
☐ Leave extra space on your desk.
☐ Use your favourite pen.
☐ Get comfortable.
☐ Eliminate factors that could hinder your creativity.

In Part 3 we'll examine how to ensure that productivity can flourish through effective communication between you and your staff.

Part 3

Communicating with Style

Effective communication between you and your staff is probably the single and most important ingredient for both short- and long-term success. This section examines the importance of emphasising objectives to your staff—be they your organisation's, your department's or your project team's. We'll also look at what you can do to foster a climate in which motivated employees can perform at their best and what steps you can take as supervisor to avoid demotivation. Chapter 17 offers advice on how to handle the data processing professional, a topic which can be of great importance to you if you have little experience in this area.

Other chapters in Part 3 focus on keeping a good thing going, working with the under-achiever and excelling in communications. Chapter 19 offers a unique system for 'improving the quality of interruptions' that you endure during the working day.

After completing Part 3 you should have a better understanding of how the timing, content, and quality of your communications affect the outlook and performance of both you and your staff.

CHAPTER 15

Emphasising Objectives

Every working day thousands of individuals are recruited, and while each may have a fair and accurate description of the duties and responsibilities for which he or she was taken on, the vast majority have no real information regarding organisational goals and objectives.

It is a mistake on the part of supervisors to think that merely discussing an employee's role will provide sufficient information for the employee to perform adequately and provide the organisation, division or department with a fair return for the money invested (eg in salary, benefits etc).

Every employee should be required to read and retain a written statement of goals and objectives. Meetings should be held regularly to discuss how the individual departments or project teams facilitate the accomplishment of the company objectives.

This chapter discusses several reasons why it is vital that your staff understand your overall objectives, as well as those of the organisation, and poses these questions:

- ☐ How can you get everyone working towards the same basic objective(s)?
- ☐ Can departments with seemingly competing interests work in unison?
- ☐ How does emphasising project goals help to demystify your behaviour?
- ☐ What one question can employees ask themselves, in your absence, that will help to guide their activities?
- ☐ Why should goals and objectives be quantified?
- ☐ Is a better directed and informed employee more productive?

All in unison

One of the easiest ways to induce an entire organisation to work towards the same basic objectives is to ensure that those objectives are known by each and every employee. When all employees understand the organisation's objectives, there is greater potential for every working minute of every day to be better directed towards those objectives. The same holds true on a project or departmental level, and in communicating with your staff.

The pay-off in pursuit of organisational objectives can be dramatic. For example, 30-minute periods traditionally wasted at the start or conclusion of each day might otherwise be used by employees to achieve that extra effort in contributing to overall objectives (also see Chapters 11 and 12).

Assembling the team

Having all employees fully aware of organisational objectives increases the effectiveness of smaller teams at the divisional or departmental level. It's far easier for employees with seemingly competing interests to be part of the larger team when the accomplishment of objectives is everyone's chief priority. By adhering to the organisational objectives, some of the perceived 'inherent' differences in viewpoint between divisions or departments will diminish.

For example, the sales division of the marketing department is keenly interested in increasing the level of sales activity in the next year. The quality control division within the production department, however, is keenly interested in producing only high quality products that pass inspection.

Based on the internal capacity of the company, the quality control division may feel that only a limited number of units of a certain product can be produced successfully. Lacking understanding of company objectives, the sales and quality control people in the above example could be forever at odds.

The sales staff and quality control staff can be united in their efforts, in the light of the company's objectives. If one of the company's objectives for the coming year is to expand the sales base, achieve a defined level of growth, and penetrate new markets, then the quality control division may need to revise their standards downwards somewhat, or arrange a meeting with the sales division to discuss the optimum level of output that the production department can achieve, in support of the sales division's compliance with company objectives.

Alternatively, if the company objective is to remain well entrenched in present markets, produce a high quality top-of-the-line product, and increase profitability on sales, then the sales division will have to adjust accordingly. This may include avoiding those customers for which sales fail to achieve a sufficient profitability level per unit sold (eg substantial delivery charges, difficult installation, or poor credit risks).

While conflicts between departments and divisions are predictable due to the nature and responsibility of the work performed, a team-like atmosphere can nevertheless be produced when all employees and all departments or divisions work towards the same ultimate objective(s).

Demystify mysterious behaviour

Informing your staff of objectives diminishes employees' perception of what appears to be mysterious behaviour on your part. This is an overlooked, real benefit. Often, employees believe that the behaviour of their supervisor is inconsistent.

You may be working in direct support of project objectives but employees that aren't aware of those objectives will not appreciate the job that you're doing.

Afford unsupervised employees better decision-making ability

Since it is usually not possible to supervise every employee daily to the optimum degree, the next best step is to provide a set of guidelines or operating procedures from which your staff can make sound decisions. With a complete and clear picture of objectives, employees can make informed decisions in the absence of direct supervision.

In essence, unsupervised employees will be asking themselves 'will this be good for the project/department/company/organisation?' when they encounter a situation for which immediate supervisory feedback is not available.

Knowing the objectives will not provide every employee with clear-cut information on how to proceed in every instance for which there is no supervision; however, in the long run, decision-making capabilities will be improved.

The need to quantify

When informing staff of objectives, make sure that the objectives are quantified when possible. It is not enough to state as an objective, 'We want to increase sales as much as possible'. Instead say, 'We want to increase sales from 108 to 132 units per year'. Thus, each employee is afforded information as to the percentage or absolute number of the increase in unit sales to be achieved. Quantifying goals also enables employees to have a better understanding of how their contribution affects the whole.

The communication and information that you receive from the bottom up, on the ease (or difficulty) in meeting quantified objectives, helps you in the role of supervisor. The feedback enables you to have a better understanding of what your tasks will be in achieving the quantified objective(s).

Not foolproof

Informing your staff of objectives is by no means a foolproof method for overcoming many of the ills that plague all organisations. However, a better informed and better directed employee will ultimately be a more productive employee. Even a minor increase in productivity at the individual level can have a ripple effect and contribute to a greater level of overall productivity and smoother and more profitable operations.

Checklist 30
COMMUNICATING OBJECTIVES

- ☐ Produce and distribute goals and objectives to staff.
- ☐ Hold regular meetings which emphasise progress towards objective(s).
- ☐ Demystify your behaviour — let your staff know what you're doing.
- ☐ Avoid assuming that your staff comprehend their objective(s).
- ☐ Quantify goals and objectives.

Can you 'motivate' your staff towards greater productivity? Since all motivation is really self-motivation, Chapter 16 focuses on what you can do realistically to assist in the process.

Motivating Your Staff

Keeping all employees 'motivated' all the time is a near impossible task. Yet, as supervisor, you are often the driving force by which difficult tasks and activities can be accomplished by your staff. It's not enough to be merely a good scheduler or administrator; you must be a good 'people' person.

Contemporary thought holds that no one can motivate another; each individual must be motivated from within. Yet we know that individuals will make an extra effort for a cause, for personal advancement or for a leader.

What then can be done to foster a climate conducive to generating that extra effort? In this chapter we'll canvass those management and supervisory techniques that enhance staff motivation and consider these questions:

- [ ] Does your enthusiasm encourage your staff?
- [ ] How often should praise be offered?
- [ ] How does delegation help in the motivation process?
- [ ] What is demotivation? Can the supervisor unknowingly cause this to occur?
- [ ] What are some characteristics of leadership?

Lead by example

Studies by Likert, Blake and Mouton and others support the notion that the participatory style of leadership is most effective in the long run. There are numerous ways to help achieve a climate conducive to a motivated staff. It is helpful to indicate your concern about your staff and maintain awareness of the individual problems and concerns of each. Encourage independent thinking, initiative, and resourcefulness. For your more competent staff members, work towards reducing the amount of supervision that they receive, thereby indicating your trust and reliance upon their capabilities.

If you are an enthusiastic type of supervisor and demonstrate this enthusiasm in your speech, mannerisms and behaviour, this enthusiasm can be contagious to your staff and will help to create a spirited atmosphere in which everyone is energised and raring to go. Remember, though, that a certain amount of pressure may be necessary with some to ensure that goals and objectives are met. Only a small minority of workers are ever challenged to perform near their true capacity.

There are other ways to get the 'motivation' ball rolling:

Checklist 31

GETTING THE MOTIVATION BALL ROLLING

- ☐ Offer praise as often as possible and certainly where the employee undertakes a late afternoon, a new, or an especially difficult assignment. As Blanchard and Johnson appropriately say in the *One Minute Manager*, 'Catch somebody doing something right'.
- ☐ Be receptive to ideas from your staff. Learn from them and be open to all suggestions, including those with little chance of working. This openness will enhance more creative thinking and more independent and happier employees.
- ☐ Demonstrate your confidence in your staff by what you say and what you do. Convey the belief that the tasks assigned can be performed effectively.
- ☐ Focus on results rather than methods for accomplishing tasks. This fosters creativity and ingenuity and keeps the team's approach to obstacles fresh and vibrant. I once supervised a person who approached tasks completely differently from me, but uniformly achieved effective results.
- ☐ Offer continuous feedback. Let your staff know how they're doing and where they stand.
- ☐ Make the extra effort. When you go out of your way to assist a staff member or incur some personal inconvenience, you are conveying a message that the success of your staff is your highest priority and that the real reason that you're a supervisor is to help them.

Raising morale through delegation

The very nature of your tasks and responsibilities demands that some decision-making authority be turned over to your staff. The ability to delegate successfully will decrease your workload while increasing the productivity and morale of those you supervise.

Many supervisors, especially first-time supervisors, fear using delegation because they don't fully trust their staff or they've always been effective at taking care of everything themselves and can't break the habit of doing it all.

It's useful at this point to review the definition of supervisor. Chapter 1 pointed out that a supervisor is one who tells people what to do and how to do it. A supervisor directly oversees the work of one or more individual employees while also maintaining many of his or her own operating duties—all in connection with the performance of a single cohesive function. Now, using this definition and acknowledging the principle of operating at the highest skill level, a supervisor's responsibility for delegation becomes clear.

Operating at the highest skill level essentially means that 'no one should perform a task that can be performed just as well by someone who is paid less'. Thus, the supervisor or manager who continues to 'do it all' and avoids delegation when a staff member could in fact handle the task is supervising poorly and is likely to be incurring higher costs for his or her department or organisation.

What, then, does the successful supervisor do to delegate effectively?

Checklist 32

EFFECTIVE DELEGATION

- [ ] Delegate to employees who show enthusiasm, initiative and interest and who have previously demonstrated the ability to handle and balance several tasks at once.
- [ ] Delegate enough authority for successful completion of the task by allowing key employees to make their own decisions, take initiative and continue operating even in your absence.
- [ ] Delegate on a piecemeal basis—ensuring that employees are able to handle effectively what has been delegated to them and do not feel that they have been swamped or over loaded. Then as competence is demonstrated, increase the complexity and frequency of the tasks to be delegated.
- [ ] Prepare your staff for delegation. This involves prior assessment of the employee's skills, interests and needs. You can even ask employees what new tasks and responsibilities they would like to assume.

☐ Spend extra time with those employees who are undertaking new challenges so that the delegation process proves effective.

Independent of your current level of delegation as supervisor, it's a good idea right now to examine all other tasks and responsibilities you currently maintain which could effectively be turned over to your staff.

Demotivation

While the management and psychological theorists maintain that we can only do so much to help 'motivate' our staff and that motivation lies within, it is possible to demotivate staff through poor practices and behaviour. Demotivation can mean any reduction in enthusiasm, initiative or output on the part of your staff as a result of something you've done.

Checklist 33

SOME DEMOTIVATING FACTORS

☐ Reprimanding or belittling a staff member when others are around (see Chapter 21, Giving and Receiving Criticism).

☐ Being preoccupied with your own activities and appearing selfish or manipulative of others.

☐ Maintaining a favourite among your staff that is obvious to everyone.

☐ Being callous or insensitive to employees' needs.

☐ Being indecisive when swift or forceful action or direction is called for.

☐ Discussing shortcomings of one employee with another.

☐ Using a staff member's employment to coerce him or her to perform a certain action.

☐ Stifling employees' expression, ideas and growth.

Many of the items cited above are elaborated more fully in Part 4, Avoiding Supervisory Pitfalls. Chapter 22, How to Tell if You're a Bad Supervisor in particular offers an in-depth look at demotivating behaviour and practices.

Supervisor as leader

An American academic has developed a leadership checklist that dovetails nicely with the supervisor's role as a motivational facilitator:

Checklist 34

THE SUPERVISOR AS MOTIVATOR

- ☐ Do I give employees adequate support?
- ☐ Do employees understand how to do the task assigned?
- ☐ Have I spelled out what's expected in terms of results?
- ☐ What have I done to cultivate a positive relationship?
- ☐ Do my staff have adequate freedom in which to work?
- ☐ What have I done to involve the staff in their jobs mentally and emotionally?
- ☐ Have employees been allowed to participate in setting goals and deciding means of achieving them?
- ☐ Have I shown adequate concern for employees as individuals?
- ☐ Have I shown adequate concern for employees' personal goals?
- ☐ Have I accurately assessed employees' strengths and weaknesses so that tasks are assigned which capitalise on strengths?
- ☐ Have I adequately and reasonably challenged my staff?

CHAPTER 17

Handling the Data Processing Professional

In the past several years the data processing professional has emerged. You may be assigned to supervise one or more of them. This chapter explores ways to ensure that this employee becomes an active member of your team.

Dick Lessar was hired by a civil engineering firm to develop a project tracking system and improve the firm's use of computer graphics. Steve Pierson was Dick's supervisor. Steve had no real background in using data processing equipment and realised that he'd have to rely heavily on Dick in this area.

Dick was not like most other employees of the company. He seemed aloof and distant, and more interested in working on the terminal than interacting with others. Dick seemed to be marching to the beat of a different drum and sometimes appeared to be lost in space just staring at the screen.

While Steve had had substantial experience in effectively supervising others, Dick Lessar posed a new problem. Steve had no idea how long specific computer-related tasks should take and thus how to best monitor Dick's activities.

What steps can a supervisor assigned to handle a data processing professional take to ensure that a team-like atmosphere and normal supervisory functions are maintained? This chapter provides such information and considers the following questions:

- ☐ How can a supervisor who is otherwise unfamiliar with data processing equipment effectively supervise a data processing professional?
- ☐ What should one look for in an effective data processing professional?
- ☐ What specific steps must be taken to ensure that the data processing professional is an active part of your project team?
- ☐ How can you spot an ineffective programmer?

A staff member is a staff member

Steve resolved that he would supervise Dick the same way that he did his other staff members. Thus, Dick was responsible for attending all staff meetings and participating in staff meetings just like everyone else. This helped to prevent Dick from becoming isolated from the rest of the project team or developing the notion that the machinery he worked with was more important than his colleagues or his company.

Reporting and monitoring

Steve recalled the case of an earlier employee having data processing responsibilities who maintained a closed, almost secretive approach to handling tasks. Steve knew that loyalty comes from being part of a team and that a non-communicative employee or one that maintained privileged information, ie a corner on the market was not healthy for the employee, the team, or the company. Thus, Steve prepared specific goals and objectives in consultation with Dick, drew up a task list and time-table and met Dick daily to review problems encountered and overall progress.

To increase Dick's understanding of the company's ongoing projects, Steve familiarised him with the current forms and controls in use and illustrated how information was handled and compiled. He also took Dick out to the field so that Dick could view first hand what was being accomplished and how his job supported company operations.

Assessing Dick's work

Steve realised that no matter how much he learned about using data processing equipment, programming and computer graphics it would take him a long time to be able to evaluate the effectiveness of Dick's efforts. So Steve set up procedures whereby he could quickly gain the information he needed regarding Dick's performance.

First, Steve requested that all programs developed be accompanied by documentation, ie an English narrative, full code printing that explained the importance of each program element. Steve also established a peer coding review system whereby Dick's programs were examined by others familiar with this area.

Steve was then able to determine if Dick was developing 40 lines of code when most other data processing professionals could accomplish the same task in say, 20 lines.

Profile of an effective DP professional

Steve read a little about managing in the computer age, talked to others and was able to produce a profile of an effective data processing professional:

Checklist 35

THE EFFECTIVE DATA PROCESSING PROFESSIONAL

- ☐ Frequently asks 'When do you need to have it by?'
- ☐ Consistently meets goals.
- ☐ Relies on systems manuals—no one on planet Earth can memorise every nuance of every instruction of software and other data processing systems support materials. Successful professionals use the manuals.
- ☐ Employs standardised modular/component programs when available—in plain English, this means no reinventing the wheel and no customised program development when adequate programs already exist.
- ☐ Relies on programming dictionaries.
- ☐ Is sharp and articulate just like other good employees. This also means avoiding using computer gobbledegook in explaining what's being done or what has to be done.

Detecting the poor data processing professional

Unfortunately, some data processing professionals cloak their ineffectiveness by inaccurately or inappropriately conveying 'hardware' shortcomings. In reality the shortcomings are, more often than not, in their own capabilities. The poor professional may be using techniques and procedures learned three to five years ago while machine capability, software and support systems have increased exponentially.

The employee who says 'I can't do this' or 'This can't be done' may really be saying, 'I don't know how to do this', or 'My background is insufficient to accomplish what you've asked', or 'The equipment may be fully capable of handling the task but I'm not sure on how to get started'.

The data processing professional who says, 'Response time will suffer' is often offering a lame excuse. The more appropriate statement may well have been, 'This will require three to five second search delays'.

One final clue to the poor professional is the continued missing of self-determined target dates. For example, in consultation with the supervisor, if the employee says that goal XYZ can be accomplished in six working days, you offer eight days, and it's still not done by the tenth day, very few excuses will justify this prolonged execution time.

There's no magic and there's no mystery to working with data processing equipment. The time required to accomplish tasks requiring high doses of creativity and innovation can be estimated much as non-DP tasks are.

In short, the notion that the data processing professional must be supervised differently from others is highly erroneous.

A good perspective by which to view the data processing function is that data processing equipment, software and systems support materials serve the business of your organisation and ultimately, human needs.

Checklist 36

SUPERVISING THE DATA PROCESSING PROFESSIONAL

- ☐ Treat the DP professional just as you treat any other staff member.
- ☐ Require that the DP professional report regularly.
- ☐ Familiarise him or her with the company's ongoing project.
- ☐ Assess his or her work (get help if you have to).
- ☐ Require that programs developed be accompanied by documentation.
- ☐ Observe his or her use of systems manuals and standardised modular/component programs.
- ☐ Recognise that statements such as, 'This can't be done' may be a cover for incompetence.
- ☐ Remember there are both good and bad DP professionals, and the good ones stand out just like other good employees stand out.

CHAPTER 18

Instilling a Team-like Atmosphere

Michael Johnstone supervised a staff of six for a property development company. Time and again Michael would toss about the problems faced by his staff, work through solutions on his own and then call a meeting to announce what would be done. Frequently Michael's solutions were right on target, clearly addressed the problems at hand and could be effectively implemented with existing resources.

One might say that Michael was very effective in supervising and coordinating the activities of his staff, yet slowly he was 'losing them'. Michael's problem—he was not involving his staff in the decision-making process. Although the staff clearly recognised Michael's ability to create viable solutions to existing problems, each staff member felt somewhat disenfranchised from the 'team' because he or she was not really able to participate or contribute to the creative problem solving process.

What steps can Michael take to continue to supervise as he sees fit while giving staff members a greater feeling of responsibility and instilling a more team-like atmosphere? In this chapter we'll explore the answers to the following:

- [ ] Why are decisions made by the team often more effective than those made by an individual?
- [ ] What immediate benefits are provided through group decision-making or brainstorming?
- [ ] Why does the supervisor essentially still get his or her way even after posing problems to the group at large?
- [ ] What should be encouraged during brainstorming sessions?
- [ ] What are some of the pitfalls of group decision-making?

Spread the decision-making load

During the next few months a few of the staff met Michael independently to discuss the need to be more involved in decisions which affected their assigned tasks and workload. Michael had been reading about the dynamics of group decision-making in a highly respected supervisory management newsletter to which he subscribed.

Having confidence in his own abilities to lead the group effectively while allowing for more staff input, Michael prepared an agenda to be distributed to the staff in advance of their next meeting.

On this meeting agenda, Michael listed many of the traditional items that appeared on earlier ones but this time also added a section entitled 'Issues to be resolved'. He then went on to list several items all posed in the form of questions, under this heading.

In the few days before the meeting, Michael noticed that his staff was buzzing a bit more than usual and there seemed to be a more highly charged atmosphere within the office.

Surprise, surprise

When meeting time came, Michael was ready as usual. However, what he didn't anticipate was that his staff was also ready in top form. The meeting was rather routine as Michael passed over the early agenda items.

When it was time to discuss 'Issues to be resolved', the meeting came alive. Mary Witherspoon, who had barely said anything in the last meeting, had a list of alternatives prepared for many of the questions posed. Keith Carter offered many suggestions. The other staff members each made a few good points during the balance of the meeting.

Michael was truly amazed. He had hoped that his new approach would encourage greater participation and achieve that more team-like atmosphere he was seeking. He was surprised that this had worked so well and so quickly.

Relying on the team

What are the benefits a supervisor can enjoy when relying on the team to approach problems creatively and resolve issues?

Some managers and supervisors fear that allowing the staff to participate in the problem-solving process will diminish or subvert the supervisor's plans and ideas on how to accomplish the project at hand successfully. This is simply not true. As supervisor you still moderate the meeting, maintain strong influence regarding ideas and opinions expressed and lead the discussions as you see fit. Rather than subvert or thwart your role, getting your team involved enhances your position.

Checklist 37
BENEFITS OF RELYING ON THE TEAM

- ☐ Group performance is increased—more participation leads to more creative thinking which often leads to more feasible alternatives.
- ☐ Poor or unworkable alternatives are more likely to be spotted—in group discussion with several minds working on the same problem, the probability of someone detecting an unworkable solution is greatly increased.
- ☐ New issues are identified—invariably discussion on how to resolve current issues facilitates the group's ability to identify other issues of potential importance. This aids the planning process, since these issues are often identified sooner by the group than if left to be discovered solely by the supervisor.
- ☐ More enthusiasm is generated—individual staff members gain an added measure of enthusiasm when approaching tasks assigned to them when they know that the group is aware of and involved with what needs to be done.
- ☐ Objectives are re-emphasised—tying in with the information presented in Chapter 15, group decision-making allows everyone to examine the issues to be resolved in the light of the group's overall objectives.

Brainstorming

One of the easiest ways to generate a high level of group participation is through brainstorming. To use brainstorming effectively, pose a question or problem to the group and then, with magic marker or chalk in hand, go up to the board and begin writing everything that comes out of the group. This is no time for qualifying any of the suggestions or recommendations offered. Simply record the ideas expressed as fast as they come and when the group feels that they have 'wrung themselves out', stop.

Now, still encouraging group participation, go back to the list of ideas presented and stratify them into three groups. One group should consist of those ideas that can quickly be eliminated because of budget constraints, resource constraints or because they are obviously impractical or unworkable. Another group should consist of those ideas that appear to be gems. You may only get a few gems but that's all you usually need. The final group can consist of those ideas presented which the group feels may have some merit but are second tier to the gems.

Prepare three new lists, one for the gems, one for the second tier group and one for the eliminated group. Now go back to the gems and discuss each one in more detail. The final solution for the issue being discussed may be formulated as a result of this group discussion, or you may have to work on this a bit more on your own. Either way, you have effectively accelerated the process of resolving issues while instilling a team-like atmosphere.

Similarly, brainstorming can be used to handle the other issues that confront you. When soliciting the group during a brainstorming session, remember no idea is too outrageous. Write them all down no matter how they sound at first hearing.

Often brainstorming sessions get a bit humorous as the collective creative energies of your staff foster a highly spirited, almost electrified atmosphere and many endorphins (positive nerve impulses) are fired. Also, one suggestion that can always be made when confronted by an issue is to do nothing. Undoubtedly someone will offer it, and it too should be recorded.

Pitfalls of the group process

There are a few things to look out for when involving your staff in the problem-solving process. First, don't get lazy. More than one supervisor has got into the habit of letting the group provide all of the real creative thinking, and then over-relying on these sessions. Another factor to consider is the strong influence of a senior, dominant, or influential group member (other than yourself) whose thoughts and ideas are reflected more often and more strongly than others on your staff.

A third pitfall occurs when the group becomes more interested in arriving at a harmonious decision rather than focusing on an innovative, perhaps controversial, perhaps untested, but highly promising approach.

It's your job to keep these sessions balanced and on target, to use the ideas and suggestions generated when appropriate but to continue to maintain control and provide necessary direction.

Checklist 38

CREATING A DECISION-MAKING TEAM

- ☐ Distribute an advance copy of your next meeting agenda to your staff.
- ☐ Include an 'Issues to be resolved' section.
- ☐ Remember that team approaches to creative problem-solving are often far more effective than an individual approach.
- ☐ Use brainstorming to encourage even more ideas.
- ☐ Avoid the pitfalls of the group process—letting the group do all the real thinking, letting a senior member dominate, or allowing the group to strive for harmony rather than effective solutions.
- ☐ Keep creative problem-solving sessions balanced and on target.

CHAPTER 19

Improving the Quality of Interruptions

Vic Morrel was the project manager of a staff of seven for a small consulting firm. As project manager, Vic's main responsibility was to supervise his staff and ensure that all project deliverables were submitted on time. Vic was an effective delegator and had taken considerable time and effort to map out a workable project plan which fully involved all of his staff.

On a daily basis, however, Vic was taking a professional beating. Each of his staff members averaged about three to five visits to his office each day for a variety of questions and issues regarding project activities. Although Vic took the time to schedule well run, informative meetings and individually talked to staff in their offices, he couldn't seem to stem the tide of interruptions that were virtually burning him out by the end of each day.

What options does a supervisor have for reducing the number of staff-related interruptions per day and improving the quality of interruptions that do have to be made?

This chapter spotlights a simple system for 'improving the quality of interruptions' while maintaining overall effectiveness with your staff, and offers answers to the following questions:

- ☐ Why is the establishment of a priority system for interruptions essential?
- ☐ How does such a system provide employees with a framework for taking action?
- ☐ How does such a system promote greater staff interaction?
- ☐ What is the greatest pay-off to you in initiating a priority system for interruptions?
- ☐ What is the greatest pay-off for the entire staff of initiating such a system?

The ten thousandth interruption

Returning to Vic's situation, the number of interruptions per day seemed to be increasing. Slowly, Vic realised that his effectiveness was diminishing. He was becoming cross and irritable with his staff and couldn't wait for the end of the day to unwind.

In the evening, at home, he would toss around ideas for reducing the number of interruptions but none of them seemed to be the answer. He had thought of closing his door for several hours each day or on particular days but was afraid that someone might be let down at a crucial moment. He considered elaborate scheduling, message and memo systems, and other exotic methods but quickly decided that they would involve a great deal of effort with, perhaps, no real improvement in operations.

A week or two passed and Vic acknowledged that he would have to come up with a solution for the sake of his staff and for the sake of his own health. He decided to keep a log of staff-related interruptions over a three-day period. At the end of three days, after carefully reviewing the log, he had the answer. Many of the questions for which his staff was interrupting him could be answered by carefully reviewing the project plan. Other staff questions could be answered by colleagues, and still other questions required a yes or no or short answer that only necessitated using the intercom.

After this careful examination of the nature of the questions asked and the resulting interruptions, Vic was ready to install his plan.

The V-4 system

Vic assembled his staff and announced that a new and innovative way for handling questions and project-related problems was going to be introduced. Vic called this the V-4 System. Here's how it works:

☐ *V-1 questions*. A V-1 question consisted of any question or concern that could be answered simply by referring to the project plan, orientation kit or project meeting notes which had already been circulated to all members of staff.

Easily 25 per cent of the questions being brought to Vic could be answered by employees on their own by consulting these readily available project materials. Upon hearing this the staff acknowledged that now and then they had been a little lazy and were using Vic in a manner that was perhaps somewhat inappropriate.

☐ *V-2 questions*. The V-2 question consists of anything a member of staff may ask which can effectively be answered by another, once again reducing the number of interruptions that Vic must endure.

One might readily observe that the V-2 question doesn't reduce the number of overall interruptions that the staff must endure — it merely shifts some interruptions from Vic on to others. This is true. However, any distribution of interruptions among and between the staff would be more equitable on a personal basis than having the supervisor bear the brunt. Upon hearing this, the staff immediately agreed that it was more equitable to resolve V-2 type questions by using other staff members.

☐ *V-3 questions.* A V-3 question consists of those concerns of employees that must be presented to Vic and for which it would be inappropriate to ask another. The V-3 question, however, could be answered by a yes or a no or in one or two sentences. Thus, the need for a staff member to walk over to Vic's office and seek face-to-face communication was unnecessary.

☐ *V-4 questions.* The V-4 question is that which, having exhausted V-1, V-2, and V-3 options, can only be resolved by a close encounter of the fourth kind—meeting with Vic in person and spending some time working out the best way to proceed.

Vic explained to his staff that he had no problem whatsoever being interrupted for V-4 type questions. In fact, he encouraged his staff to consult him personally any time that a V-4 question was encountered. The key here is that after exploring V-1, V-2 and V-3 options, less than 2 per cent of all questions fall into the V-4 category. Thus Vic was effectively able to reduce the number of interruptions per day from between 20 and 35 to between 3 and 8.

Benefits of the V-4 system

Let's step back now and examine the benefits of the V-4 system. First, it provides the staff with a framework for taking action. In accordance with the recommendations made in Chapter 15, Emphasising Objectives, the V-4 system enables your staff to continue making progress even in your absence.

It also helps to promote greater staff interaction and more sharply defines your role to the staff. When you are no longer observed as the 'den mother' that handles every little question and concern, you provide your staff with the opportunity to appreciate more fully your proper role as supervisor and the importance of your time.

The greatest benefit to you is that your time is effectively increased while not markedly diminishing anyone else's. With fewer small interruptions, your creative thinking and planning time has been increased.

Later, Vic enrolled in an evening course on stress management so that he could understand better how to keep himself in top form.

Checklist 39

THE V-4 SYSTEM FOR REDUCING INTERRUPTIONS

☐ V-4—for those questions and concerns that you *must* answer in person.
☐ V-3—those items that can be handled via the office intercom.
☐ V-2—those items that can be handled by colleagues.
☐ V-1—those questions and concerns that are addressed and readily available in project related materials.
☐ Enrol in a course on, or read about, stress management.

Chapter 20 investigates the successful supervisor's role and communication in Working with the Under-achiever.

Working with the Under-achiever

Ted Knowles was supervisor in a large division of a major insurance company. Most of the employees that Ted supervised were well-adjusted, veteran employees of the company with whom he had a fine working relationship. There was one employee, however, Ted found hard to understand. Dennis Sanders was unhappy most of the time, maintained what Ted felt was a poor professional attitude and, on occasion, had a lower level of performance than many of his colleagues.

Ted felt strongly that it was within Dennis's potential to become a good employee and a satisfactory performer. In addition, Ted resolved that, as supervisor, it was his responsibility to get to the root of Dennis's problems, for the good of Dennis, the company, and himself.

This chapter is a case history of events that actually occurred and the list below shows what steps Ted took to improve the situation. (The names used have been changed.)

Checklist 40

IMPROVING THE UNDER-ACHIEVER

☐ Identify short- and long-term goals.
☐ Establish formal authority.
☐ Assign new responsibilities.
☐ Instil confidence.
☐ Maintain an environment of mutual respect, and provide career development opportunities.

Investigate first

Over the next several weeks Ted made extensive efforts to tactfully investigate possible causes for Dennis's behaviour. Ted learned that Dennis felt unchallenged in his present position which he had occupied for over four years. Dennis also had a desire for more independence and increased responsibility, something that previous supervisors had failed to acknowledge.

While Ted was not exactly new, he had been with the organisation for two years, he also learned that Dennis tended to resent new symbols of authority—anyone who had been with the company for fewer years than Dennis.

As if these problems weren't enough, Ted also discovered that Dennis had a pronounced lack of self-confidence and self-esteem and fostered the notion that management and colleagues had low confidence in him. Combined with Dennis's self-admitted poor communication ability, the portrait of a very unhappy and unproductive employee emerged.

Turning the tide

The story of Dennis Sanders is not so unusual; surveys point to widespread worker discontent and maladjustment in contemporary business. The challenge facing Ted is not uncommon either though many supervisors never accept the challenge of helping a losing employee to adopt winning ways.

Let's examine a variety of methods for achieving optimal performance by a hitherto under-achiever.

Identify short- and long-term goals

The employee needs to clearly identify specific short- and long-term goals for him or herself and work with management on what needs to be done to achieve them. It is possible that the employee has no goals, only vague goals, or has lost sight of any goals that were originally established. This situation is like having a ship without a rudder that ultimately founders. It is the supervisor's responsibility to sit down with the employee and formally set goals in writing and plan steps to reach those goals in detail.

Establishing formal authority

Ted's authority as supervisor had never formally been established in Dennis's mind. In large part this is often due to the fact that neither the previous supervisor, nor top management had ever issued a written directive defining the formal working relationship. As simple as this procedure may seem, it is often necessary before some employees can ultimately accept a change in supervisors.

In addition, many employees need to comprehend their place in the formal structure of the organisation or, specifically, the division, and to see where they stand in relation to new staff. A sense of insecurity can arise from having an uncertain status and the unhappy employee has a special need to be informed.

New and appropriate responsibilities

Dennis wants more responsibility and more independence, yet suffers from poor communication ability and interpersonal skills. This suggests that he is task-oriented as opposed to people-oriented. The supervisor should present as many different challenging tasks as the employee can handle in this situation.

The question arises, however: are these tasks available in Dennis's current position? As changes occur within the division and throughout the organisation, an employee who remains relatively stationary must be afforded new and challenging tasks lest he feel that the world is passing him by.

Instil confidence

The supervisor must praise the insecure employee more often and more clearly. The employee should always know when he or she has done a good job and be given feedback as soon as possible. A couple of compliments a day from the supervisor can keep the doctor away.

It should also be made clear to the employee in a private session or staff meeting that the supervisor does have confidence in the employee and expects the employee to maintain the good performance standard and good attitude of which he or she is capable.

Defuse the time-bomb

It would be over simplistic to suggest that Dennis's personal and professional problems will simply float away through proper supervision. There are steps that can be taken, however, to diffuse an employee's confrontational, abrasive mannerisms. The supervisor, leading by example, should turn the other cheek, ignore unwarranted remarks, and strive to maintain an environment of mutual respect. Hostility must be met with patience and fairness along with the aforementioned praise whenever possible.

Large doses of patience and understanding do not, however, mean that disciplinary standards be dropped. If an employee arrives late, spends excessive time on the phone, takes long lunches, and engages in otherwise unproductive practices, the correction of these deficient habits is a step towards improvement in other areas.

Onward and upward

It's also important that the employee be informed as to the quickest road for advancement and more responsibility. The employee must be informed that by increasing his or her level and range of skills he or she increases potential for career advancement and earnings.

Employees that keep doing the same job well year after year usually end up feeling they're in a rut. The employee must be encouraged to get cracking—open up those training books, attend those courses and *volunteer* to take on new or extra assignments.

Clean up your own backyard

The supervisor must continue to approach the goals and objectives of the division with enthusiasm, all the while displaying eagerness in working with the unproductive, unhappy employee. The supervisor who maintains negative thoughts about interacting with this employee will not be able to disguise these thoughts effectively and this will put a damper on the relationship. The employee will sense it and respond negatively.

Converting a losing employee to a winner requires nothing less than the erasure of all negative thoughts the supervisor may hold, replacing them with a positive attitude and visible enthusiasm towards the employee. In short, the supervisor leads the employee instead of the other way around.

Saving an employee on a sinking ship is no easy task. Moreover, no management system or school of thought has yet devised a fool-proof method for dealing with unhappy, low-performance employees.

CHAPTER 21

Giving and Receiving Criticism

Ruth Decker supervised a staff of eight in the personnel department of the local authority. Robert Hodges was the youngest and most recent addition to her staff. One week, Ruth had to attend a management training programme out of the office and needed Robert to finish a report for the divisional director by the time she returned at the end of the week. Over the telephone, Ruth very carefully outlined for Robert what needed to be done and how she could be reached if he ran into problems.

Two days later, on Wednesday, Ruth had not received a call from Robert and thus assumed that he was encountering little difficulty in undertaking the assignment. Ruth returned mid-afternoon on Thursday and was pleased to see Robert's typed, finished report on her desk ready for review and, she hoped, ready for submission on Friday.

After just a few minutes Ruth realised that Robert had missed the mark on some of the points made in the report, had completely left out one small section and had prepared a poor conclusion. Given that the report was to be delivered the following day, Ruth was rather upset.

Her immediate reaction was to take the report over to Robert's office and in strong language ask why he hadn't sought help and why the report had the various shortcomings. Report in hand, she marched in the direction of Robert's office and stopped a few paces from the door. Robert was discussing a new task with another of Ruth's staff. Ruth looked at her watch, noticed it was about 3.30, and headed back to her own office.

Coolly and calmly thinking through the situation, she decided that the report was indeed salvageable and that in an undisturbed 45 to 60 minutes she could probably shore up its weak points, resubmit it to the typing pool and still have it available Friday morning.

About an hour later she was finished and the report was ready to be retyped. She made an extra copy which reflected the changes that she added so that her subsequent discussion with Robert would involve mild criticism mixed with supervisory assistance.

In this chapter we'll review both giving and receiving criticism and provide answers to the following:

☐ What is the best time of the day and week to criticise employees?

☐ When should you never criticise?
☐ Where should the criticism be offered?
☐ What are some effective ways to handle criticism levied at you?
☐ How can you handle the chronic complainer?

Criticising without crushing

Ruth finally got together with Robert on Friday morning and reviewed his report paragraph by paragraph. Ruth pointed out the strong points and the weak points and left Robert with a copy. She then emphasised that, although it was not desirable to issue the assignment by a long distance telephone and to follow up by the same method, it's what the situation called for. She explained to Robert that by calling for assistance while the report is in progress everyone saves time.

Robert agreed that what she said made sense and that he would follow her directions more closely in the future. By handling the situation in this manner Ruth was able to provide constructive criticism to Robert that both conveyed her present concerns, offered assistance and established a solid working relationship for the future.

Let them have it early

Numerous management analysts agree that the best time to dispense employee criticism is early in the day and early in the week. This affords the opportunity to speak to the employee again some time during the day in a more casual, lighthearted way to assure the employee that everything is all right, that you criticised the performance or behaviour, but not the person, and that you have confidence in the employee's ability to continue to handle or assume responsibilities.

Criticising late in the day poses several problems. First, you may end up sending an employee home who's worried or anxious about his or her job—unnecessarily so. Also, you and your staff are often tired at the end of the day and any criticism or strongly worded message can be taken out of context or overblown because of the fatigue.

The same holds true for the employee whom you criticised just before a weekend or holiday.

Cool down

There's an old Chinese proverb which says, 'Never write a letter when you're angry'. An analogy when dispensing criticism could be 'Never criticise when you're angry'. Use whatever delaying process you can to put time between when you initially feel the need to criticise an employee and when you actually do it. You'll be more objective, your criticism will be more constructive and your overall employee communications will be vastly improved.

Conversely, don't wait too long to dispense the criticism after the poor performance has been identified. As with justice, criticism is best dispensed quickly.

Criticise in private

The reason why Ruth stopped on her way into Robert's office was that someone else was there. Ruth instinctively knew that it was inappropriate to criticise Robert in front of another staff member and not enable him to have the benefit of a quiet, extensive, closed-door session in which his viewpoint could be aired. Ruth also knew that discussing one employee's shortcomings with another was a disguised, malevolent form of criticism. Conversely, she was quick to praise, particularly in the earshot of others, and thus was perceived as a supervisor who communicated with style.

Receiving criticism

You're not the only one who feels the need to criticise. On occasion, your staff does too. Their criticism is often muted, concealed or disguised in the form of a suggestion. Whether you call these criticisms, complaints, grievances or suggestions, author Ray A Killian offers a four point system for receiving criticism.

Checklist 41

RECEIVING CRITICISM

---

1. *Be courteous*. Treating an employee courteously while he or she is offering feedback greatly affects his or her attitude. One way to convey your concern is to take notes of what is being said and then repeat the essential elements so the employee is assured that you have full comprehension. You may even wish to thank the employee for

full comprehension. You may even wish to thank the employee for bringing this item to your attention and let him or her know that you'll give it fair consideration.

2. *Gather information.* Review the complaining employee's record, if only to determine that the employee is not a 'chronic complainer'. Is he or she absent, non-productive, uncooperative or a poor performer? Realistically, this will colour your perception of and reaction to the problem addressed.

3. *Take appropriate action.* If the criticism or suggestion is justified, tell the employee what you intend to do to improve the situation. If the complaint is unjustified 'be firm and calm in telling the employee so'. Another possibility exists: the suggestion or criticism made could be focused on something that cannot be changed. This may take some doing, but attempt to explain why this is so.

4. *Follow-up.* When the employee's grievance or suggestion was valid and helped you better to execute your responsibilities or helped the department or organisation in some way, let him or her know in at least a week or two. Often that which is suggested by employees can improve overall efficiency.

James O MacDonald, in *Management Without Tears*, offers some suggestions on handling chronic complainers. MacDonald advocates a put-up or shut-up approach. This involves asking the complainer to 'prepare a written analysis of the problems and to propose solutions'. If the complainer doesn't follow through you can then convey the message that next time 'a written analysis will again be requested'. If the complainer does submit a written analysis it can then be evaluated on its own merits.

The hallmark of a successful supervisor is being able to give and receive criticism effectively. It has been said that 'You're as big as what irritates you.' If you let the small grievances and complaints of your staff get to you, and every member of staff has them, then you'll overreact and needless spend energy on brush fires, while missing forest fires.

If you establish a supportive, cooperative framework in which criticism can be both dispensed and received then you'll be perceived as an effective communicator and a highly effective supervisor.

Here's a review of the key points made in this chapter:

Checklist 42

GIVING AND RECEIVING CRITICISM

- ☐ Criticise early in the day and early in the week.
- ☐ Avoid criticising when you're angry.
- ☐ Listen to what the employee has to say.
- ☐ Dispense the criticism as swiftly as possible.
- ☐ Criticise in private and let the employee have a chance to explain.
- ☐ Be courteous when handling employee complaints.
- ☐ Take notes of what's being said and then repeat essential elements to assure full comprehension.
- ☐ Gather information to determine if the employee is a chronic complainer.
- ☐ Take appropriate action, ie change and explain, explain if the complaint is unjustified, or explain if nothing can be done and why.
- ☐ Follow up on the employee complaint a few weeks later by thanking him or her if operations have been improved.
- ☐ Handle the chronic complainer with a put-up or shut-up approach.
- ☐ Establish an environment in which both giving and receiving criticism can occur without being disruptive.

This concludes Communicating With Style. In Part 4, Avoiding Supervisory Pitfalls, six chapters are presented to help guide you past potential problems that may occur as a result of your management style.

Part 4

Avoiding Supervisory Pitfalls

Supervisory pitfalls are easy to fall into. Since the perfect manager has never existed, at least some of what you do and how you do it is going to generate problems with and for your staff. Chapters 22 to 27 cover a wide area of supervisory pitfalls. Chapter 2, for example, How to Tell if You're a Bad Supervisor, offers nine ways to examine the way you supervise to check if you're making it difficult for others and if you're being perceived as a bad boss.

The other chapters, such as Failing to Listen, Supervising Out of the Office, and Undermining the Ideal Employee offer unique and in-depth insights into the problems that may occur in the demanding and challenging role of supervisor. A host of checklists and guidelines are provided that will enable you quickly to take the steps necessary to avoid, or get out of a supervisory pitfall.

CHAPTER 22

How to Tell if You're a Bad Supervisor

There are hundreds of books and articles that tell us how to supervise or manage better, and how to get the most out of employees. This chapter focuses on how to tell if you're a bad boss—what behaviour, procedures and style you may be propagating inadvertently that may demotivate staff, reduce overall productivity or otherwise cause employees to regard you as a 'bad boss'.

Topics presented will include the practice of maintaining fairness and consistency, exploiting your staff, offering the continuing promise or the dangling carrot, and making light use of heavy terms.

This chapter will help you to come to grips with some poor practices that may be dividing you and your staff. Questions to be answered include:

- ☐ Why does mistreating one employee make you lose out with all the rest?
- ☐ Why is no promise better than a continuing one?
- ☐ When should terms such as 'teamwork', 'dedication' and 'commitment' be used?
- ☐ What phrase indicates that you're bowling googlies to your staff?
- ☐ Is flexibility important, and if so why?
- ☐ What three elements must be balanced for the supervisor to be effective?

Unfair to one, resented by all

If you strive to maintain consistency and fairness with all your staff except one or a few within your organisation or department, you can quickly lose the respect of all. Strive to be consistent and fair with 100 per cent of your staff. Most employees have a built-in sense of what is right and strongly dislike the ill treatment you may bestow upon a colleague (independent of the circumstances).

You would be better off as a supervisor, literally, to be unfair or inconsistent with all employees occasionally than with a select few regularly. Carefully review your employee roster now and assess whether each one receives the same treatment. If not you may be deemed a bad boss.

Exploitation

On company-related trips, do you always make employees drive? My boss in my first management consulting firm literally gave me responsibility for all clients beyond a 30-minute drive, irrespective of the nature of the work or my ability to handle the assignment. Little wonder my car averaged 25,000 miles per year and I was always exhausted. Do you require your staff to commit personal time and resources in executing tasks that you're not willing to commit yourself in handling your responsibilities? If so, you may be creating a work environment in which employees feel that they're being exploited.

Granted, as supervisor or boss with far greater responsibility than that of any employee whom you supervise, it is important to optimise or effectively allocate scarce resources—namely, your time—while on the job. However, if you establish a standard which you personally do not live up to or you devise policies to facilitate disproportionate convenience for yourself, you may soon find yourself on the 'bad boss' list.

Offering the continuing promise

A frequent trap that many supervisors fail to avoid is offering a continuing promise to employees. By continuing promise, I mean the hint or outright declaration that a more favourable future is in store for some or all of your staff if they accomplish X,Y,Z.

Offering a promise to employees is not in itself necessarily a bad management practice. Offering a continuing promise that is not fulfilled but re-offered after original goals or favourable outcomes have been reached reflects poor management. That should be avoided at all costs.

Ask yourself, 'Do I habitually make promises to employees that I don't keep or that I can't keep on time?' It is far better not to promise anything, than to break or not keep a promise. One exceptionally effective supervisor lived by what might be a familiar credo—'Never promise more than you can deliver, always deliver more than you promised'.

The dangling carrot

Closely related to continuing promise is the dangling carrot. Do you find yourself asking more of employees just before they're due for a rise or annual holiday? This is a form of coercion which many employees find irritating, or worse, bitterly resent.

The good supervisor attempts to maintain an even keel and a balanced workload for employees throughout the year and doesn't resort to cornering them at opportune times.

Light use of heavy terms

Some supervisors get in the habit of adopting management or corporate buzz words to try to motivate staff but really don't believe in or practise the declaration being made. For example, do you urge your staff to show loyalty to the department or organisation while displaying none yourself? Do you ever count on or ask for the friendship of employees while not truly being a friend at all?

Use of these terms and other high-minded expressions or concepts such as 'commitment', 'teamwork', 'team spirit' and 'dedication' mean very little spoken to employees when they are actually outside the bounds of your own management style. If you find yourself resorting to platitudes when supervising employees, there's a good chance of turning them off.

Programming for failure

A particularly heinous practice is to programme your staff for failure. This is characterised by making assignments that can't be completed successfully or by not providing sufficient guidance or resources that would assist the successful completion of the task assigned. Smart employees know when they've been programmed for failure and try to take action to obtain the guidance or resources needed before a crucial deadline is missed or an important project botched.

If you're in the habit of doling out assignments that have built-in time bombs, you'll quickly develop a poor reputation.

Bowling googlies

When you communicate with your staff, do you bowl googlies, that is alter the meaning of something that you said previously? Poor supervisors are in the habit of 'bending' what was assigned or said to suit their own current need. The same boss that gave me all the long road trips also had the nasty habit of changing instruction in mid-stream and vehemently denying that any change had been made. Have you ever felt like wanting to tape someone to catch them in their own inconsistency? Believe me, I have wanted to.

If you find yourself continuously saying to employees 'that's not what I said' or 'that's not what I meant', you may be a spin bowler without knowing it. Such a supervisor is particularly troublesome for employees who are often not at liberty to explain your error to you or to challenge your method of giving and following up on assignments.

Carved in stone

The other extreme is being overly rigid when issuing assignments or maintaining work schedules. In the changing work place of the eighties many employees need flexibility in both the hours that they work and the order in which assignments are due.

The supervisor who arbitrarily clings to traditional schedules that are not based on any true organisational, departmental or personnel needs will quickly be deemed inflexible by the staff.

Zero feedback

Are you in the habit of informing your staff of departmental or organisational developments only when the news is good or when it's convenient or advantageous for you to do so?

One is reminded of the story about a 12-year-old who had never spoken in his whole life. His parents took him to doctors, but no one could find anything wrong. One morning his mother burned the toast and overcooked the eggs at breakfast. Whereupon the young man jumped up from the table and said, 'This breakfast is terrible'. His parents were aghast and asked why he had never spoken before. The boy replied, 'Up till now everything was okay!'

Employees have a right to learn of developments which may impinge upon their jobs or performance. Some supervisors, however, provide or withhold information as it suits the supervisor and not necessarily as it is needed to foster an atmosphere of trust and cooperation.

Employees need to hear of negative developments as well as positive ones. Granted, this does not mean that you are duty or honour bound to report to your staff instantly everything that occurs. However, if you maintain a policy of consistently withholding information, particularly when your staff end up gaining at least partial information from secondary sources, the 'bad supervisor' tag will soon be on you.

It's your choice

One can choose to appease employees or latch on to what's popular to avoid being labelled a bad boss. However, there is a more important reason for you as supervisor to avoid the bad boss designation and that is that your ability to work with, motivate and further develop your staff will be directly related to the respect and feeling that your staff have for you. Therefore, from a purely pragmatic standpoint, a good supervisor must balance what he or she wants to do, knows is right, and knows will enhance the greatest long-term departmental or organisational benefit.

Here's an important checklist of behaviour to avoid:

Checklist 43
BEHAVIOUR TO AVOID

- ☐ Being unfair or inconsistent to one employee.
- ☐ Requiring more of your staff than you yourself would do or have done.
- ☐ Offering a continuing promise.
- ☐ Tempting an employee with a 'carrot' before salary review time.
- ☐ Using terms you don't follow or believe in.
- ☐ Programming your staff for failure.
- ☐ Retracting what you said, or altering it later.
- ☐ Being inflexible.
- ☐ Providing little or no feedback (see Chapter 23).

The next chapter challenges your listening capability—something on which we all can improve.

CHAPTER 23

Failing to Listen

Listening is such a rare commodity in society that the Sperry Corporation effectively built its image by positioning itself as 'the company that listens'. It is said that on average, people spend 45 per cent or nearly half of their communication time listening. Good listening is an active, complex process that requires knowing a few basic tenets and lots of practice. In a personal or professional relationship, it pays for both to sharpen listening skills.

Few managers/supervisors, or people in general for that matter, have thought about learning how to become a good listener. We get distracted when someone is talking, jump ahead in our minds to what we want to say next, and later blame the speaker for not getting the message across.

Let's learn how to become better listeners, to 'listen legibly'. This chapter will provide answers to the following:

- [ ] What does active listening involve? (Hint: a one word answer.)
- [ ] Why don't we listen as well as we could, and should?
- [ ] If you 'drop out' of a conversation are you likely to catch up later?
- [ ] How much faster can we think than speak?
- [ ] What is the most positive, rewarding combination of non-verbal responses that we can offer a speaker?
- [ ] Does location affect our listening capacity?

Listening involves work

Dr Mortimer Adler of the Aspen Institute, in his highly respected book *How to Speak and How to Listen*, says active listening involves work. Although listening occupies more of our time than speaking or reading, Adler says we seldom receive any training in this area.

Why don't we listen as well as we should? Dr Chester L Karrass, Director of the Santa Monica, California-based Center for Effective Negotiating, offers several reasons:

Checklist 44
WHY DON'T WE LISTEN?

- [ ] We often have a lot on our minds and it's not easy to switch gears quickly to fully absorb and participate in what is being said to us.
- [ ] We have adopted the habit of talking and interrupting too much and do not let the other party continue, even when it may be to our benefit.
- [ ] We are anxious to refute what the other person has said and, if we do not do so readily, we are afraid that we may forget to make our point.
- [ ] We allow ourselves to be easily distracted because of the setting or environment in which the meeting takes place. Have you ever asked your secretary to hold all phone calls during meetings?
- [ ] We jump to conclusions before all the evidence has been presented or is available.
- [ ] We discount or 'write-off' some statements because we don't regard as important the party who is presenting them.
- [ ] We tend to discard information that doesn't match what we want to hear or that we don't like.

Dr Karrass points out that 'poor listeners often drop out of a conversation in the hope that they will catch up later. This seldom happens'. If you find your mind wandering while listening, make a conscious (and repeated, if need be) effort to focus on the conversation.

You're not alone

If, by now, you've confessed to yourself that you're not a good listener, lighten up—you do not have a monopoly on underdeveloped listening skills. Virtually all human beings, especially supervisors, must work to improve their listening skills. Because we are able to think and process thoughts four to five times faster than the normal speaking rate, it is easy to let our minds race ahead of the speaker, not focus on what is being said, or appear uninterested. The faster our ability to process information, the greater the potential for our display or practice of poor listening when an oral presentation is being made to us. Good listeners use this lag time to make mental summaries of information presented and notes of ideas to pursue later without losing focus on the conversation.

Visual cues can be highly influential in interpersonal communication. Facial expression and eye contact are two of the most important visual cues. For example, if you avoid eye contact while listening, this could communicate disapproval or lack of interest. Even if you look directly at someone, your facial expression may still indicate a negative reaction. Probably the most rewarding combination is a smiling face and a head nod in combination with direct eye contact.

From these and other cues we infer support, confirmation, and agreement. A good way to enhance one's capability to listen is to pick a location and a time (when possible) that is free from noise and interference when listening to someone (or some media message).

Also, as an exercise, try speaking to one of your staff for several minutes with a tape recorder on. Then play back the tape. You may be quite surprised at what you missed.

Here is a checklist developed by Dr Richard C Cupka to help you evaluate your own listening habits:

Checklist 45

EVALUATE YOUR OWN GOOD LISTENING HABITS

( ) Do you give your staff a chance to talk?

( ) Do you interrupt while someone is making a point?

( ) Do you look at the speaker while he or she is speaking?

( ) Do you impart the feeling that your time is being wasted?

( ) Are you constantly fidgeting with a pencil or paper?

( ) Do you smile at the person talking to you?

( ) Do you ever get employees off the track or off the subject?

( ) Are you open to new suggestions or do you stifle them immediately?

( ) Do you anticipate what the other person will say next? Do you jump ahead, anticipating what his or her next point will be?

( ) Do you put the employees on the defensive when you are asked a question?

( ) Do you ask questions that indicate that you have not been listening?

( ) Do you try to out-stare the speaker?

( ) Do you overdo your show of attention by nodding too much or saying yes to everything?

( ) Do you insert humorous remarks when the other person is being serious?

( ) Do you frequently sneak looks at your watch or the clock while listening?

This is a tough checklist and anyone who is honest with him or herself will undoubtedly discover several areas for improvement.

Becoming an active and effective listener provides two other important benefits:

- You may gain information from new sources that would previously have been missed due to poor listening.
- Even if you don't agree with the other person, at least he or she will feel that you gave him or her a fair shake.

Developing good listening habits is one way to become a better communicator. Active listening improves your interpersonal skills and human relations capabilities. Good listening can enhance your personal and professional life. The sooner you start listening effectively, the better. You hear!

Checklist 46

A SUMMARY OF GOOD LISTENING

Good listening:

- ☐ Takes work.
- ☐ Means not 'dropping out' and trying to catch up later.
- ☐ Is a universally rare capability.
- ☐ Can be exhibited by smiling, nodding and looking at the speaker.
- ☐ Is enhanced by a location free from noise and interference.
- ☐ Helps to develop our overall communication capabilities.

Another pitfall to avoid is not keeping your staff informed of both good and bad news that may be of concern to them. Chapter 24, Practising Paternalistic Supervision, deals with this issue.

Practising Paternalistic Supervision

Despite breakthroughs in management theory, the paternalistic supervisory manager can still be found stalking the corridors of business and industry. The paternalistic supervisor tends to treat his or her staff like children. While it is necessary and recommended to inform employees of both good and bad developments within the organisation, the paternalistic supervisor will often provide information only on good developments, shielding employees from news or information that is deemed less than good.

This chapter expands on the 'zero-feedback' portion of Chapter 21. By consulting this chapter, you'll obtain answers to the following:

☐ Why do some supervisors avoid disseminating information on bad developments?
☐ How does 'telling it like it is' help the supervisor?
☐ How can you quell rumours and reduce speculation quickly?
☐ What might you get after disseminating the news? (Hint: a one word answer.)

Give yourself a chance

In observing the phenomenon of the paternalistic supervisor, the story comes to mind of the teacher who is told on the first day of school that this term's students are slow learners and lack enthusiasm. After only a few minutes in the class on the first day, sure enough, the teacher confirms the original report. Such is the case with the paternalistic supervisor.

If the supervisor believes that his or her employees are unable to accept and handle both good information and bad, then the same situation is being created as in the the classroom example. The teacher who treats the students as slow learners with no enthusiasm never really knows their learning capacity and potential for enthusiastic response, given a proper learning environment. Likewise, the supervisor will not know if employees can handle information on bad developments because he or she has never disseminated such information and given the employees a chance to respond.

Many supervisors will argue that disseminating information on bad developments does more harm than good. This is simply not so—if handled properly, a wide variety of benefits may be derived by the supervisor, the employees, and the organisation. Moreover, the danger of not relating the bad news, or misinforming, generally propagates rumours and overreaction on the part of the employees, which can create unnecessary harm and anxiety. Many an inaccurate rumour has leaked out of companies, often on to the business pages of the newspapers, all because some highly misinformed (or worse, never informed) employee came to some outrageous conclusion and then overreacted.

What are the benefits of treating employees like adults—of informing them of both good and bad developments of the company? Let's examine them in detail.

Gain respect

When employees are treated like adults and given information that is of importance to their careers and well-being, the supervisor gains respect. In an era of oversell, overpromise, and underdeliver, employees respect the candour of a supervisor who is able to 'tell it like it is' and goes easy on the sugar coating.

Rolling with the punches

Providing employees with adverse information helps to prepare them to develop a framework for rolling with the punches. Over time, they will come to realise that some bad company news is part and parcel of being in business and must be taken in the proper context: the organisation has undoubtedly survived time and again, and bad news and adverse developments are often temporary.

Part of the team

Employees who are treated like adults and are provided with accurate, relevant information by their supervisors and upper management tend to feel more like part of the team (also see Chapter 18), trusted members of the company, and equals in mature response to adverse situations. Noted team productivity and team building specialist Robert Bookman, president of Bookman Resources, has encouraged and observed the development of this phenomenon many times. 'Office mates', says

Bookman, 'who feel like they're part of the same team, tend to develop a collective "we can handle it" attitude.'

Less down time

The fastest way to quell rumours, reduce speculative conversation on the state and direction of the company, and get people back into a productive mode is to provide the facts as they develop.

It is ironic that most managers have a hard time facing employees when bad news must be disseminated. Yet this is the very time at which management must exhibit its ability to lead. It is easy to present good news, but it takes guts to present bad news.

Less bitterness

In those cases when the news is very bad and includes lay-offs, the supervisor or manager who has kept employees abreast of organisational developments will encounter far less bitterness and resentment if, in fact, some employees must be laid off. If this does not seem like a significant benefit, rest assured that if the time comes when you must lay off employees, having kept them informed will be of tremendous benefit.

A chance to prepare intelligently

One very good reason why employees must be kept informed is that they deserve a chance to prepare intelligently for at least short-term developments within the organisation. Many people don't like surprises of any nature, let alone of ill fortune. For those supervisors who are concerned that informing employees of bad developments may cause unnecessary anxiety, wasted time etc, consider how much anxiety and wasted time will occur if news is in the form of rumour or innuendo, or how much time will be lost if management drops an information bomb and expects employees to carry on as if they had been kept advised all along.

A chance to help

Finally, and this is by far the most important benefit of informing employees of company developments, consider the tremendous pool of human resources that your employees represent. Through their collective capabilities (whatever developments are currently plaguing the company, and hence necessitating the need to present bad news), the employees may, through greater productivity, suggestions, volunteering, or other methods, help to reach a solution.

Witness the strong employee support at Chrysler as chronicled by Iacocca. This possibility is in itself sufficient reason to let your employees know about company developments and to treat them like adults.

Checklist 47

BENEFITS OF AVOIDING PATERNALISTIC SUPERVISION

- ☐ Gain respect of employees.
- ☐ Develop a team that can roll with the punches.
- ☐ Reduce down time.
- ☐ Reduce bitterness—if very bad news is forthcoming.
- ☐ Provide employees a better chance to prepare.
- ☐ Induce staff support.

Now let's read Chapter 25 to see what harm is caused by issuing late afternoon assignments.

CHAPTER 25

Issuing Late Afternoon Assignments

Albert Harrison was a good, fast worker. His ability to manage his staff and turn out well crafted, voluminous weekly reports and other documents was marvelled at by all—except the word processing department. You see, Albert's timing was atrocious. At any minute of the day, including the last one, he was likely to unload his work.

Unless you have tasks to assign that simply must be completed by the next morning, it is unwise policy to issue assignments after 4.00 pm on a working day. If the assignment you must issue is of an emergency nature, then of course, any time of day will have to be sufficient for handling the emergency. However, for non-emergency and non-urgent work, issuing a new assignment to an employee late in the day can only cause problems in the long run, and reduce your credibility as a capable supervisor.

In this chapter we'll examine some of the reasons why issuing an assignment late in the day is undesirable. Specifically, these questions will be answered:

- [ ] What is the immediate impact on most employees receiving a late afternoon assignment?
- [ ] What does frequently issuing late afternoon assignments indicate? (Hint: a two word answer.)
- [ ] Why is the practice ill-timed from a productivity standpoint?
- [ ] Name some desirable alternatives.
- [ ] What should you bestow upon any staff member who successfully executes your late afternoon assignments?

Ladies and gentlemen, start your day!

Most employees have their day planned, whether informally or formally, and receiving a new assignment within 30 to 60 minutes of departure can disrupt whatever order and serenity they have finally achieved from accomplishments until 4.00 pm.

Many days your staff may be so busy that issuing a new task in the late afternoon can only add to the tension and strain that had already been developing. Other times, when your employees may not be fully occupied, the issuing of a late afternoon assignment can be met with mild panic.

It should be stressed by all means that employees have the responsibility to perform their duties faithfully and follow the direction of their managers or supervisor. However, each employee likes to feel that he or she has some semblance of control over the work environment. Doling out an assignment to someone late in the afternoon shatters any precept of control that an individual may have.

Directly related, issuing late afternoon assignments may yield a pronounced increase in an employee's anxiety and can induce long-term insecurity about the working environment. We all need psychic space and time in order to perform adequately. Being summoned into the manager's office late in the afternoon and told of new and added responsibilities increases the anxiety of most employees.

Obviously, some employees thrive on activity and are eager to tackle new assignments at any time of the day or night. In your own organisation you are probably already aware of who these people are and how to best use them. For the majority, however, doling out assignments after 4.00 pm serves no good purpose and will eventually undermine your effectiveness as a supervisor (also see Chapter 9, Supervising Cycles of Productivity).

Is this necessary?

Examining the issue from a supervisory standpoint, if the assignment is non-emergency or non-urgent, then assigning it in the late afternoon can indicate poor planning on your part. This is particularly true if you know that the employee to whom you are assigning this new task is already immersed in another project that will not be finished for at least several days.

Many employees, justly or unjustly, also believe that the supervisor who doles out assignments late in the afternoon is demonstrating poor planning and/or supervisory skills. Thus, late assignments are often received and completed with a slight sense of resentment by the employees.

How much can really be accomplished?

A very important question you should ask yourself before doling out a non-urgent, late afternoon assignment is, how much can really be accomplished on the day the assignment is issued? Can an employee who is about to depart in 30 or 60 minutes adequately comprehend new instructions for completing this assignment, read any available literature, or make any in-roads towards completion?

For most people productivity is generally highest in the morning and is understandably lower in the late afternoon of the working day. Thus, from a productivity standpoint, it makes poor (if any) sense to dole out assignments late in the afternoon unless it is absolutely necessary. In general, employees will be less motivated, more fatigued, and less likely to plunge into the new assignment with enthusiasm.

In issuing an assignment late in the afternoon, what could be your real objective? Do you, as supervisor, feel a pressing need to get things off your desk and on to the desks of others? Do you sincerely believe that the half hour or hour that an employee may be able to expend on a new assignment will be the most effective and efficient use of his or her time? That same boss who sent me on the longest trips also made a point of loading me up (down!) with assignments in the last three minutes of the day before my holiday started! Think twice before handing out those late afternoon assignments and the operations of your plant or division may run smoother in the long run.

Desirable alternatives

While it is not recommended that assignments be issued late in the afternoon, it is entirely recommended that assignments be introduced, to be started the next day, later in the week or some time in the immediate future.

In this respect, the employee can be 'oriented' in the right direction and be able to integrate this new assignment into his or her plans. You may provide or suggest background material to read or analyse, sources of information including phone numbers to ring or individuals to write to.

It is helpful to provide a rough outline (as discussed in Chapter 12) or working plan on how the assignment is to be handled, mentioning that this will all be discussed again later in more detail.

It is also recommended that you *ask* an employee if he or she can handle a quick assignment or if he or she can restructure his or her plans at short notice to add this assignment to other professional responsibilities. Most good employees, when asked to take on an additional assignment late in the afternoon, will respond affirmatively as they are often eager to show the boss a willingness to make the extra effort, or they actually do have sufficient slack time in which the new assignment can be handled or initiated.

Praise them to the hilt

Finally, be sure to give lavish praise to any employee who successfully handles late afternoon assignments. This will help to reduce an employee's anxiety about receiving such assignments in the future and will help to create an environment where, if necessary (or even if not necessary for that matter), you will periodically be able to issue late afternoon assignments successfully.

In the long run, avoiding the allocation of new assignments late in the afternoon will be best for everyone.

Checklist 48

AVOID GIVING LATE AFTERNOON ASSIGNMENTS

They:
- [ ] Disrupt employees' personal cycles.
- [ ] Add to employees' stress and anxiety.
- [ ] Are not often necessary.
- [ ] Are perceived as poor supervision and/or planning.
- [ ] May not yield adequate return.
- [ ] Are contrary to peak productivity periods.

If you can't avoid issuing late afternoon assignments, here's a summary on how to handle it best:

- [ ] Offer the assignment as an introduction.
- [ ] Supply supporting materials.
- [ ] Ask employees if they can absorb a new assignment.
- [ ] Offer lavish praise.

Now let's look at the insidious habit of assigning or monitoring employees outside the office.

CHAPTER 26

Supervising Out of the Office

Jim Roberts had come into work early one morning so that he could finish a project that required a few final touches. By 11.30 a.m Jim had accomplished great deal as the project was completed that morning. Near lunch time, Jim took the lift down to the main floor and was about to cross the road to get a sandwich when he passed his boss, Jack Simmons.

Jack was preoccupied, and hadn't really noticed Jim when he passed by with a big 'hullo'. Jack managed to say, 'Hullo, Jim' and then walked on for a few steps, when he turned around and said in a louder voice, 'One moment, Jim.' Jim retreated into the main lobby to hear what Jack had to say.

'I've got some figures I'd like you to check, and also the Walker Company report from last month should be revised, and also blah, blah, blah . . . .'

Is this scene all too familiar? In this chapter we'll answer these questions:

☐ How widespread is managing/supervising out of the office?
☐ Why do supervisors frequently commit this sin?
☐ Is supervising out of the office a time saver?
☐ How do collared employees feel?
☐ Why is it harmful for a supervisor to always be Mr or Ms Business?

Let's continue now with what happened between Jack and Jim.

I can't hear you

By the time Jack had finished his monologue, what he was saying really didn't matter too much to Jim. You see, Jim had put in a good morning's work and was now on his way to lunch, and while he would normally be ready to tackle any assignment given him, at this particular moment he was simply not interested.

When Jack finally finished, Jim almost inaudibly muttered, 'Okay, must grab a bite to eat'. He then made his way to one of the sandwich bars with about one-tenth of the enthusiasm of several minutes ago.

This situation, unfortunately, occurs thousands of times every working day. Jack and Jim have a fairly sound working relationship and it is not Jack's intention to demoralise Jim. Nevertheless, discussing assignments and responsibilities during chance meetings in the lobby of the building or the sandwich bar is of no benefit to anyone.

Why does an otherwise professional, well-meaning supervisor often forget that there is a proper time and place to discuss work assignments and job responsibilities and that the discussion of either of the above at the wrong time or place can demotivate or dampen the spirits of the most loyal and hardworking employees?

Many reasons

One reason why a well-meaning supervisor may inadvertently and inappropriately 'collar' an employee outside the office or on otherwise 'neutral' ground is that he or she simply happens to think of the task at the moment an employee was passing and didn't wish to lose that particular train of thought. Occasionally, we all have thoughts which we feel we'll forget unless we express them immediately.

For the supervisor, however, discussing or issuing an assignment on the spur of the moment can only reflect poor plannng. The actual number of times when a particular employee must be informed of a task or a responsibility on neutral ground is, in fact, minimal. Assuming the employee is doing his or her job, and the manager has effectively coordinated planning responsibilities, no employee should have to be collared in the lobby or washroom unless there is a company emergency, or the supervisor has ample justification for doing so.

Some supervisors who practise such a technique mistakenly believe that discussing an assignment in the stairwell is a time saver. Nothing could be further from the truth; most employees will not be mentally prepared to hear your message. Thus, if you provide instructions at the wrong time, you're likely to have to repeat them.

If I had a pound for every time I encountered someone doling out instructions to someone else in the men's room, I still wouldn't get rich. But the scene take place frequently, and if it weren't so irritating, it would be comical.

Often, supervisors who give instructions outside the office proper may do so because they believe it is part of their job, or consistent with the role that they must maintain. This belief is also fraught with illusion; always appearing as Mr or Ms Business to those that one must supervise establishes a superhuman standard which ultimately cannot be maintained. There is nothing wrong with letting employees know that you are human, that you do not think solely about business all day long, and that you possess the ability to 'come down from the mountain' at least occasionally.

Nothing else to say?

Many supervisors who dole out assignments at inappropriate times engage in such action because they have nothing else to say even though they recognise that this behaviour is not recommended. This is a tragedy of interpersonal communication. If, when passing an employee whom you supervise, you can think of nothing else to say besides 'The XYZ report has to go out next Tuesday', then you are in serious trouble.

If you are at a loss for words when passing an employee, you might try commenting on the weather that day, praising an article of the employee's clothing, or just saying, 'hullo' and leaving it at that. If the 'cat' has really got your tongue, you can even just nod or smile— anything but resort to playing supervisor in the streets.

Finally, supervisors who dish out assignments in the main lobby are totally insensitive to the employee. These supervisors may think, 'Oh, it's okay', or 'Joe Smith takes everything in his stride', or 'Sally knows that I know she's a good worker'. These assumptions are simply unfair. It is important to remember that, as supervisor, your words hang heavy on an employee's mind. William A Marstellar said it best in *Creative Management*: 'Everyone who works for you is afraid of you to one degree or another'. For you to discuss a task in the lift might indicate to the employee that the task is of considerable importance, that the employee has not been effective lately, or that something else is wrong.

How do they feel?

From an employee's perspective, being given an assignment at the wrong time can contribute to an atmosphere of constant pressure. An employee may soon feel that there are not even minor periods of rest on the job: just push, push, push for greater efficiency or higher productivity. The employee who feels that he or she is always 'on the treadmill' will start to be absent more often, will not volunteer for as many tasks as before, or may begin to prolong present tasks. I once surveyed several dozen people on this issue and *no* one likes it, although a few said it was occasionally acceptable.

Many employees will believe that you are insensitive to their needs. It is both helpful and necessary that some moments of the working week be not filled with new instructions. Many times after an employee has put in a good morning's work and is heading for lunch, the noon break becomes much more important to him or her than otherwise. It is not merely a time for nourishment; it is also a time to readjust psychologically to forthcoming tasks and responsibilities.

In one sense, a lunch break, upon completion of an important project, can even provide a similar 'lift' to a week's holiday.

Care to know what an employee will think of you if you maintain the practice of collaring him or her on neutral turf? He or she is eventually bound to believe that you lack the fundamental skills of a supervisor. If employees are already aware of the project or task that you are discussing, they may also believe that you are absent-minded or at least forgetful.

Another strong reason why one shouldn't manage in the streets is that it is patronising. Have you ever got into a lift where a supervisor was apparently giving instructions to an employee as they proceeded to the ground floor at the close of a day? It is not a particularly exhilarating scene, and almost makes one want to say, 'Enough, save it for tomorrow' directly to the supervisor.

Checklist 49

NOT MANAGING OUT OF THE OFFICE

Avoid:
- [ ] Giving instructions.
- [ ] Issuing new assignments, and
- [ ] Reminding employees of responsibilities while in the street, in the lobby, in the lift, or in the washroom.
- [ ] Strive to avoid these practices first thing in the morning, near lunch time, or late on Friday.

You'll be perceived as a better supervisor and your interpersonal communications will improve. Most importantly, however, your employees will be better motivated and happier.

CHAPTER 27

Undermining the Ideal Employee

Wendy Hughes works long and hard. She gets things right and is an employee who can be relied upon. Why would Wendy encounter significant problems as a result of her efforts?

Do you supervise an 'ideal' employee, someone who comes to work on time, willingly puts in overtime, does what is delegated to him or her, always gives 100 per cent, and often a little more, is loyal and a definite asset?

Often the employee that follows the boss's requests diligently, shows loyalty, eschews gossip, and consistently puts in a full day's work, arouses the jealousy and suspicion of colleagues and the supervisor! Regardless of the 'ideal' employee's intentions, many are ready to believe that the employee is a crawler or sycophant.

In this chapter we will explore the supervisory pitfall of contributing to the undermining of an ideal employee, and answer the following:

- ☐ What are some of the reasons why supervisors may be suspicious of ideal employees?
- ☐ Why are colleagues suspicious?
- ☐ How do salary problems foul up good employees?
- ☐ Do ideal employees get taken for granted?
- ☐ What is the Persian Messenger Syndrome?

Suspicious supervisors

Believe it or not, many supervisors are suspicious of an ideal employee and are, in fact, actively seeking 'clues' as to why the employee is doing such a good job. The supervisor may have known or worked with a previous employee who also exhibited a high achievement level and sound fundamental business skills, only to learn that this person

1. was preparing to start a business of his or her own;
2. was using the experience to obtain a new better paying job in another firm; or
3. was camouflaging his or her real interests which were contrary to the objectives of the organisation.

Thus, as the 'ideal' employee continues to work harder to impress his or her boss, a greater degree of suspicion may ensue. There are also many employees that do not give a full day's work, who do not follow their supervisor's requests, and who are not willing to give their 'all'. When they encounter someone that does an outstanding job, defence mechanisms don't allow them to believe that the 'ideal' employee is, in fact, doing an excellent job.

Since, in most businesses, cooperation and team work is needed to produce a synergistic effect that leads to success, the ideal employee (because of subtle ways that colleagues practise ostracism), often ends up doing many tasks alone or concluding that it would be easier to go his or her own route in completing projects. Thus, the unobservant supervisor may regard the employee as 'not a good team member'.

Underpayment

The ideal employee naturally assumes that he or she can look forward to an uninterrupted, increasing stream of earnings. He has been, after all, highly efficient and effective in contributing to the total profitability of the firm.

A problem can result when it's time for a rise and the employee, knowing full well how hard he or she has worked feels exploited when the increase is less than expected. The supervisor on the other hand, may feel that the increase in the employee's remuneration has been determined fairly. Thus, an ideal employee may be 'ideal' only for a time, being defined as that period in which he or she is earning income commensurate with the contribution.

Exploitative supervisor

Far too often, an ideal employee is exploited by the supervisor. This is characterised by increasing assignments without increasing recognition, of the waving of the proverbial 'carrot' (see Chapter 22) for an extended period, or negating or not properly recognising continuing contributions that the employee has made.

All of the above can also be viewed as 'taking the employee for granted'. This is a costly mistake for supervisors in that the ideal employee is often recognised, unfortunately, after departing the organisation.

One partner in a solicitors' office confessed (after the event) that he had employed the world's best legal secretary and because she was so good, thought there was no end to the volume of work he could pile on to her. There was an end—she departed for the same pay under less exploitive circumstances.

Under-use

Sometimes an employee is so good on the job that the chances for increased responsibility are diminished because the supervisor is reluctant to make the change. Thus many 'ideal' employees can often find themselves under-used despite doing an excellent job.

Potential inability to look out for oneself

Finally, let's examine how an ideal employee can run into trouble on the job because he or she is unskilled in self-protection techniques. The Persian Messenger Syndrome is one situation that confronts many employees. The syndrome got its name because in ancient times, the King of Persia was known to reward those messengers that brought him good news and to cut off the heads of those messengers that brought bad news. Naturally, this prompted most messengers to bring only good news.

The inherent difficulty here is that the messengers who should have been rewarded were those that brought bad news, because it's more difficult to bring bad news. The king, of course, didn't separate the messenger from the news that he was bringing.

Unfortunately, the Persian Messenger Syndrome exists today in large measure throughout business and government. The ideal employee, upon preparation of a financial report or a numerical analysis may decide that the dissemination of bad news is necessary.

By candidly presenting the information, or by not reducing the degree of the bad news (through careful use of adjectives), even an 'ideal' employee may be stepping on a land mine if the supervisor falls prey to the syndrome. This is but one example of many ways an ideal employee's inability to cover him or herself can produce negative effects.

The examples cited above illustrate that, through minor misunderstandings, defence mechanisms and other factors of distortion, even an 'ideal' employee can run into trouble on the job.

Are you guilty of any of the following?

Checklist 50

UNDERMINING THE IDEAL EMPLOYEE

- ☐ Being suspicious of good workers.
- ☐ Supporting ostracism by colleagues.
- ☐ Supporting an inadequate recompense arrangement.
- ☐ Waving the proverbial carrot.
- ☐ Under-using and then holding back a key staff person.
- ☐ Impersonating the King of Persia.

Avoiding supervisory pitfalls, upon which Part 4 has focused, is in many ways the flip side of communicating with style.

In Part 5, we'll plunge headlong into Tackling Problems Professionally.

Part 5

Tackling Problems Professionally

In this section we'll examine some tough problems that are bound to come your way and how to tackle them professionally. Chapter 28, Laying the Groundwork for Redress, will give you the proper perspective and action steps necessary to deal effectively with the problems discussed in the chapters that follow.

The chapters are presented in increasing order of the severity of the problems you may face until Facing Up to the Fear of Firing, Chapter 34. Chapter 35, Helping the Battered Employee, represents departure from the progression and examines a little discussed, frequently occurring problem in today's workplace.

As a result of completing this section you'll gain a simple yet workable framework for handling situations that have traditionally caused supervisors the most grief.

CHAPTER 28

Laying the Groundwork for Redress

Ideally, you supervise a small staff of highly motivated, professionally oriented employees who can respond to 'one minute' praisings or reprimands and who provide few real problems that require disciplinary action. Realistically, on occasion you may need to deal with significant problems such as high absenteeism, moonlighting and dishonesty.

This chapter lays the groundwork for tackling these tough problems professionally. The principles and procedures discussed here will be re-emphasised in the chapters that follow.

The chances are your company or organisation already has an established policy to deal with these more serious problems. However, organisation policy provides little comfort when you're on the front line daily and will most likely be the first to identify unacceptable behaviour, approach the offending employee, and initiate or recommend action.

This chapter explores the following questions:

☐ Can a policies and procedures handbook ever effectively govern all employee activity?
☐ What is an effective approach to gaining the confidence of an employee whom you must discipline?
☐ Should a record of infractions be kept?
☐ How can you ensure that each of your employees understands what is expected of him or her?

An impossible task

No set of policies and procedures, rules or job regulations will ever effectively govern all human interaction and activity that transpires at the workplace. It is an impossible task for your company or organisation to produce a document that will fairly and completely describe how to proceed in each possible instance in which an employee behaves unsatisfactorily.

More important than a thick policies handbook is the ability to assess a problem objectively, devise strategies for improving the situation, inform the employee what is expected of him or her and the penalties for non-compliance.

Gaining their confidence

In Chapter 21, Giving and Receiving Criticism, tips were offered on how and when to approach employees on problems related to job performance. Many of those tips also apply here. However, the nature of problems related to behaviour and non-productive activity require more delicate, yet assured handling.

A good way to win the confidence of the offending employee is by describing the problem to him or her as one that you both have to work at solving. It's best to start on the problem right away, avoiding chit-chat, and to gather information by encouraging the employee to speak. Also, avoid talking about the problem while standing—sitting reduces the chances of increased tensions or hostility. If possible, be seated next to the employee as opposed to across the table or desk. This also helps to symbolise that you are on his or her side and decreases the possibility of confrontation. By developing an emotional bond to honest discussion, you can help to influence the employee more favourably.

A system for constructive discipline

By approaching the problem in a professional, controlled manner you can actually increase morale rather than decrease it. This is because the employee is often well aware of his or her unacceptable behaviour and perhaps dreads the time when they would be confronted by you or some other authority. Your demonstration of professionalism, objectivity, and understanding can be a catalyst in the employee's decision to eliminate the inappropriate behaviour and take great strides towards improving the situation.

Checklist 51

HOW TO TACKLE PROBLEMS PROFESSIONALLY

1. Be certain that any organisational policy and procedural guidelines that do exist are acknowledged by your staff.
2. Highlight or display established policy or your policy regarding specific activities which may be occurring, but are inappropriate or forbidden.
3. Seek the help of your boss or a colleague to gain an added measure of objectivity and impartiality before confronting an employee.
4. Provide employees with immediate feedback when infractions of company policy have been made. Even small transgressions are important, because if they're not dealt with they often lead to greater problems later.
5. Keep a log or chart of inappropriate behaviour or activity which can serve as the necessary documentation if the situation grows worse and severe penalties are warranted, namely termination.
6. Administer a reprimand or punishment on a progressive basis— the more frequent or serious the transgression, the greater the penalty, leading up to termination.

Don't play ostrich

Inexperienced or first-time supervisors sometimes have trouble dealing with serious personnel problems. The worst thing that can be done, however, is to pretend the problem doesn't exist or to look the other way to avoid a confrontation and the responsibility to administer corrective action.

In a large insurance agency, there is a 31-year-old employee who has been dying to get fired for the last two years. He is habitually late, unenthusiastic and occasionally insubordinate. His dishevelled appearance and lackadaisical approach to his job are dead giveaways, yet no one has approached him regarding his inappropriate performance or demeanour.

By laying the groundwork or establishing a system to deal with problems in advance, you reduce the chances of being caught unprepared to deal with the issue. By knowing company or organisational policy, by communicating what you require as supervisor and by maintaining sufficient documentation or gathering sufficient evidence on inappropriate behaviour, you can dramatically limit the stress and anxiety of all concerned.

Checklist 52

LAYING THE GROUNDWORK FOR REDRESS

☐ Remember, no set of written guidelines will ever effectively govern all human interaction in the workplace.

☐ Gain the confidence of individual members of staff by working together to solve a problem.

☐ Demonstrate your professionalism when dealing with a problem.

☐ Devise a simple system for handling problems which includes highlighting policies, providing immediate feedback, keeping a log of inappropriate behaviour, and administering reprimands or punishment on a progressive basis.

☐ Don't avoid problems by playing ostrich.

In Chapter 29 we'll discuss a most insidious problem in scheduling for productivity—absenteeism!

Dealing With High Absenteeism

Today's the day you're going to accomplish great things. There are three reports that are nearing completion, two new projects to be started and you feel ready to go! Unfortunately, three of your eight staff have phoned in to report sick. Now it's doubtful that very much will get done today.

Your organisation's policy on absenteeism, lateness, and reporting should be a fundamental part of the new employee orientation procedure (see Chapter 8) and laid out expressly in the policies and procedures guide. As supervisor, however, it makes sense to re-emphasise this immediately prior to recruitment and shortly after an employee begins work. Absenteeism is very costly, and the disruption in your department's work flow can be both irritating and disheartening. You probably can't afford to be absent from your job. Some of your staff believe they can.

In this chapter we'll highlight what can be done at the supervisory level to deal effectively with the problem of excessive absenteeism and help you to answer these questions:

☐ Who is most often absent and why?
☐ Do major sports events contribute to absenteeism?
☐ What techniques have been proved ineffective?
☐ Are most employees surprised when they learn how they compare with others?
☐ What six steps effectively combat absenteeism?
☐ What is 'push' policy?

What do we know about absenteeism?

Research conducted over the last several years reveals predictable patterns of absenteeism across a wide spectrum of business and industry. Checklist 53 casts light on this phenomenon.

Checklist 53

FACTS ABOUT ABSENTEEISM

- ☐ Emotional factors are involved in 25 per cent of all absences.
- ☐ Skilled employees are absent less than unskilled or semi-skilled workers.
- ☐ Most absenteeism is concentrated in a small segment of the work population.
- ☐ Long-service, older employees are absent less than the 'under 25' group.
- ☐ Approximately 5 per cent of all one- and two-day absences precede or follow otherwise legitimate time off for holidays or weekends.
- ☐ There is a high correlation between employee 'illness' and major sporting events.
- ☐ About 3 per cent of employees are practically never absent.
- ☐ Absenteeism increases with prolonged overtime and extended working weeks.

What doesn't work

Surprisingly, warnings to high absentee workers are seldom effective. Productivity consultant Mitchell Fein points out that the person who's absent is doing what he really wants to do—not come to work (even though he may lose wages, receive punishment, and upset productivity)—and he has the right to do what he wants. But he should do it elsewhere. His personal liberty shouldn't impinge on the rights of others. Fein also maintains that efforts to reward employees to maintain good attendance has little effect, because only the good employees pick it up. Moreover, good employees still have to work harder because their colleague fails to show up (and thus be non-productive). Responsible workers have little influence over the irresponsible to show up regularly.

What then, does work?

Reducing absenteeism

A basic approach to reduce absenteeism is to keep good records on absences, study them to ascertain the pattern of absences, and discuss them with each employee. What are the reasons offered for being absent?

Often employees are surprised when they see how their six-month record of absences compares with others.

Excessive absence and lateness are a reflection of morale. To find the underlying causes of high absenteeism requires finding out how the offending employee views the company, his or her career, and specific assignments. Chronic absenteeism requires strong measures (see Checklist 55 on 'push policy').

Techniques used in various industries for reducing absences include:

Checklist 54

TECHNIQUES FOR REDUCING ABSENCES

- ☐ Avoiding payment for holidays when an employee is absent on the day before or after the holiday.
- ☐ Screening new employees closely and not taking on those with questionable attendance records at other companies.
- ☐ Requiring that the employees must talk to their supervisor when phoning in to report sick.
- ☐ Ensuring that supervisors phone employees' homes on the day of an unreported absence to check the reason.
- ☐ Tying attendance records to promotion.
- ☐ Establishing a written policy for absenteeism, and indicating the disciplinary action which will be taken if absenteeism becomes excessive.
- ☐ Altering pay days to that day in which the greatest number of employees are absent—usually Monday.

Now let's examine a strategy used by one company for handling absenteeism.

Checklist 55

THREE PARTS OF A PUSH POLICY

---

1. *Verbal message.* Upon initial interview, both before and shortly after engagement the employee should be told the company's policy

regarding absences. The employee should be told that everyone works together, that he or she is part of a team and the company or organisation. The absentee policy and phone-in procedure are made a *work rule*; it is a condition of employment.

2. *Written notice.* When an employee has been absent the supervisor must establish whether the absence was excusable or not. If inexcusable, the employee should be given a written notice that only two unexcused absences will be tolerated, at the maximum. The supervisor maintains the burden of determining the true cause for the absence, and if the absence is found to be legitimately excusable, to acknowledge it accordingly.

3. *Suspension/Discharge.* If an employee has been inexcusably absent *twice* in a six-month period, a face-to-face meeting between the supervisor and employee should be held immediately to decide whether the employee should continue. Three inexcusable absences in a six-month period constitute a reason for discharge. This must be handled in accordance with the requirements of employment legislation on dismissals.

Does the push policy sound tough? It is. But remember, marginal employees, those that contribute the least, cause the most headaches. So, why court them?

In Chapter 30 we'll meet a type of employee who has not been absent a great deal, but might as well be.

Dislodging the Employee Turned Institution

Jason Woodling has been with ACME Supply for eight years. He plays golf with the branch manager's nephew and has accumulated two and a half months of paid holiday. Jason's voice has a commanding tone. His office is near the rear exit. And Jason hasn't done an honest day's work in about three years.

There exists in many large organisations an employee who has effectively ceased functioning in the role or position for which he or she was orginally engaged, or to which the employee has been promoted. This type of employee has become what will be termed an 'institution'.

An employee who has become an institution within an organisation is acclimatised to all the ways of getting through each working day, contributing as little as possible, while maintaining an appearance of being 'on top' of the job.

The phenomenon of the employee turned institution occurs frequently throughout government bureacracy (both local and national) since it is difficult to remove an employee from such a position. However, business and industry also have their share (of institutions).

In this chapter we'll take a hard look at this problem and address these questions:

- [ ] What are some of the reasons an employee becomes an institution?
- [ ] Why are older employees more likely to become institutions?
- [ ] What prevailing conditions usually exist when an employee has effectively chosen the institution route?
- [ ] Name four ways to detect an employee turned institution?
- [ ] What are the ways to stop them?

How does it start?

An employee may become an institution for a variety of reasons. Sometimes the employee is related to someone in upper management, although the actual occurrence of this is minimal. Another reason is that the employee possesses specific knowledge or skills that the organisation cannot readily acquire from other sources. The employee may have developed a particular expertise that, at least periodically, is of vital importance to operations.

Frequently, an employee turns institution within an organisation simply because he or she is allowed to, and no one (not even the supervisor) is aware of, or willing to expose, the employee's general lack of dedication and limited effectiveness on the job.

Sometimes an older employee who has been with the organisation since 'way back' can intimidate others with less seniority. Surprisingly, this intimidation may even extend to his or her supervisor.

In order for an employee to become an institution within any organisation he or she has to fully 'know the ropes'; he or she must be able to understand how the system works before it can be circumvented. Hence, an employee cannot become an institution until gaining wide exposure to the system and its procedures.

Perhaps the employee worked for a time in the invoicing department, was transferred to sales, and then later transferred to credit control. In government, he or she may have spent time in the public relations office, acted as a special assistant to a director or worked on a special task force.

Usually, an employee could not turn institution without a lack of awareness on the part of one key supervisor or manager. In other words, there is one key person within the organisation, who, with knowledge of the employee's true work habits and operating procedures, should not allow such a practice to exist.

How to spot them

One clue that an employee has become an institution is a pronounced lack of flexibility; the employee is vitally interested in maintaining the status quo and regards change as a major enemy of the kingdom he or she has established.

The employee–turned–institution also promotes mediocrity, and when confronted with an idea from a peer or subordinate that might be good for the organisation but which would also involve real work, will often respond with idea-killing phrases such as 'we've tried that before' or 'that never works'. I knew of one person who used these kinds of statement to ward off any new assignments or responsibilities that he might have been given.

'Institutions' are also very adept at 'covering your behind' techniques and, in fact, have developed an entire set of procedures to 'cover' themselves rather than truly accomplish anything for the organisation. Some of the techniques used to cover oneself include faithfully filling out time sheets, completing other reporting requirements and quickly responding to memos and directives of immediate supervisors.

My least productive staff member, not coincidentally, was always the first to turn in his magnificently complete timesheet.

Influence peddling

Other ways to identify 'institutions' is to observe who is influence 'peddling'. There is a high tendency among employees–turned–institution to influence others within the organisation. Frequently, 'institutions' will be leaders of employee organisations or union groups, as they often recognise that these positions will shield them from having to maintain job-related responsibility.

Many leaders of employee groups are effective as employees within the organisations for which they work. The employee–turned–institution, however, uses employee or union groups for selfish ends. He or she also seeks the loyalty of other selected subordinates and tries to form a cadre of employees that will act as a buffer to 'hostile' parties.

Also, the employee–turned–institution is, more often than not, keenly aware of the benefits and deductions from his or her payslip, and uses compensatory time, sick leave, and annual leave to full personal advantage. While the employee may make no significant contributions, rest assured that he or she will be well informed of organisational policies and procedures, and will do what he or she can to stretch the policies for personal advantage.

How to stop them cold

The employee–turned–institution can only flourish when an otherwise good manager or supervisor refuses to see the true picture or to take corrective measures. The employee–turned–institution must be stopped cold, before he or she has a chance to:

Lower productivity;
Unfavourably influence other employees;
Demoralise other employees; or
Tarnish the organisation's image to outside parties.

Once an employee–turned–institution has been uncovered, quick action must be taken. First, it is desirable to reassign the employee to a new department, division, or operating unit, to reduce his or her 'comfort level'. If the transfer is not in the best interests of the organisation, then the employee should be given new tasks and responsibilities, while assigning previous tasks to someone else.

The employee–turned–institution should always be physically relocated to a different office. Preferably, the new location should be next door to you or in a highly visible spot.

Without making it obvious, you should initiate the practice of periodically checking to see how (or what) the employee–turned–institution is doing. If necessary, new (or expanded) daily and weekly reporting logs can be introduced.

Circulate a memorandum to your staff, stating that activities and behaviour that interfere with the primary functions of the group or organisation will result in punitive action or dismissal. Good employees won't be troubled reading this memo; employees–turned–institutions will cringe (if indeed they recognise themselves!).

If an employee–turned–institution is discovered after a relatively short time, sometimes a stern message delivered in person by you or the head of the organisation can rectify the situation. However, if an employee–turned–institution has been allowed to flourish for a prolonged period, has been discovered, and the seven steps above have been ineffective dismissal, unfortunately, is the best procedure. Some supervisors may find dismissal or termination too harsh. It isn't; not for someone who has consistently circumvented the system for his or her own ends. (Any such dismissal must be arranged in accordance with correct employment legislation, unless you are prepared to face an industrial tribunal for wrongful dismissal.)

Beware, the employee–turned–institution is everywhere.

Here's a review of how they get started and how to neutralise the employee–turned–institution.

Checklist 56

THE EMPLOYEE TURNED INSTITUTION

How they get started
- [ ] Maintain specific or unique skill.
- [ ] Are allowed to.
- [ ] Related to someone higher up.
- [ ] Have been with the organisation a long time, have seniority.
- [ ] Know the ropes.
- [ ] Benefit from unaware, intimidated or ineffective supervisor.

How to spot them

They:

☐ Fight to maintain status quo.

☐ Promote mediocrity.

☐ Cover themselves.

☐ Become influence peddlers.

☐ Are keenly aware of benefits policy.

How to neutralise them

☐ Reassign to new department.

☐ Assign new tasks or responsibilities.

☐ Relocate them (preferably next to you).

☐ Check on them often.

☐ Issue an expanded reporting form.

☐ Circulate a memo forbidding such practices.

☐ Deliver a stern message.

☐ Dismiss them.

Now let's look at another insidious supervisory problem in Chapter 31 – handling moonlighting on the job.

CHAPTER 31

Moonlighting on the Job

A growing portion of employees' theft of time on the job is in fact due to secondary income activities. Any secondary income activity that one of your employees engages in while on the full-time job will be termed 'moonlighting on the job'.

There are four compelling reasons why moonlighting on the job is detrimental to your department as well as the entire organisation and must be eliminated.

In this chapter these four reasons will be discussed and the following questions answered:

☐ How can moonlighting on the job reduce performance beyond the obvious loss of hours worked?
☐ Are moonlighters likely to engage in conflict-of-interest types of activity?
☐ What damage is done to your honest employees?
☐ What are some effective guidelines for handling moonlighting (not on the job)?

Reduces performance

If John Clark is scheduled to work 40 hours for his employer and instead devotes two hours each day to his own business, he is, in essence, providing 32 hours of work for his employer. However, the 32 hours he does provide are usually not a quality 32 hours.

In addition to the eight hours that John steals per week working on his own activity, his activity also takes up John's time at home on week nights and, perhaps, on weekends too. Thus, John's employer loses two ways:

1. By not getting a full 40-hour working week while paying for one, which effectively is the same as giving John a salary increase; and
2. By not getting quality hours for those hours that are being worked.

Use of organisational resources

It is very likely that John, in support of his outside business activities, will use his employer's telephone, a fair amount of office supplies, copying paper and the copy machine, and maybe even postage. While it is possible to control the unauthorised use of office supplies, the control system is often much more burdensome to all. Also, John's use of these resources may result in their short supply or in increased delays for those who are doing the job they were engaged for.

Conflict of interest

John's other activity, apart from the time he's stealing from his employer and possible use of his employer's resources, may also represent a conflict of interest. If John's outside activity has nothing to do with his employer's, then perhaps this is not a problem area. However, it is reasonable to assume that John's outside activity may be a function of his principal activity and requires similar education, background and training.

Not every incidence of moonlighting on the job represents conflict of interest. However, it only takes a few that do to make a bad problem horrendous. A direct conflict-of-interest activity should be met with dismissal (see Chapter 34).

Unfair to other employees

Perhaps most importantly, John's preoccupation at work with outside business activities is grossly unfair to fellow employees who put in a fair eight-hour working day after working day and devote their time, energy and skills to the tasks for which they were hired. Many employees who get wind of the situation may feel demoralised because John is 'getting away' with something, yet they won't expose him because they don't want to 'rat'.

Moonlighting on the job is not restricted to marginal employees – some of the most talented, high achieving, promotable employees partake in this practice. Supervisors should not consider it an activity undertaken only by marginal employees. Everyone in the organisation is a candidate.

Guidelines for moonlighting

While moonlighting on the job is insidious to any organisation, moonlighting per se may not be. 'Moonlighting is a natural and reasonable response to the complexity of employment and should not be swept under the table,' says Thomas P Ference, professor of management and director of the master's degree programme for executives at Columbia University's graduate school of business. 'It should be dealt with professionally like any other aspect of business.'

If your organisation hasn't established policy on moonlighting or if you need to personalise communication with your staff in this area, here are some guidelines from business and financial writer Bruce W Fraser:

Spell out the conditions under which you approve, disapprove or will be neutral towards moonlighting. You may applaud an employee who teaches at a college or lends skills to government schemes but disapprove of work for a firm that is in some sense a competitor.

Also, state whether in-house telephones, copy machines, secretaries or computers can be used for outside purposes. Employees may, for example, be allowed to take calls related to moonlighting ventures during the day but not allowed to use a company computer or secretary in their moonlighting.

Be clear about the job-performance that is expected from the employee so that both employer and employee can judge accurately whether performance is being affected by moonlighting.

Here's a checklist on the harmful effects of not containing moonlighting on the job:

Checklist 57

MOONLIGHTING ON THE JOB

- ☐ Effectively gives the culprit a rise.
- ☐ Reduces overall performance of and quality hours worked by the employee.
- ☐ Consumes organisational resources.
- ☐ Fosters conflicts of interest.
- ☐ Demoralises other employees.

Here are the guidelines for moonlighting policy:

- ☐ Deal with it professionally.
- ☐ Spell out the conditions of approval and disapproval.
- ☐ Cite proper and improper use of company resources.
- ☐ Spell out expected job performance.

In the next chapter, we'll continue to look at tougher and tougher problems: employee dishonesty.

CHAPTER 32

Cracking Down on Dishonesty

Employee theft and other dishonest behaviour, which includes anything from pilfering office supplies to repeatedly using sick leave as extra holiday, are thought by some to be due to an employee's perception that the employer is not interested in his or her welfare. The sociological implications and rationale for dishonesty in the workplace are beyond the scope of this book. However, in this chapter we shall explore the following questions:

- ☐ How much does employee dishonesty cost businesses each year?
- ☐ What are the reasons for the persistence and universality of the practice?
- ☐ What can you do to prevent employee dishonesty?
- ☐ How can you spot employee dishonesty?
- ☐ What should you do once you've discovered employee dishonesty in your company?

The costs

Employee theft and dishonesty is a tough problem that doesn't go away by ignoring it. It's difficult for any manager to contemplate that his or her employees are stealing time, money, supplies, or company secrets. Once becoming aware of dishonesty among their staff, many supervisors take it as a personal affront as well as a damaging blow to the company itself. A look at some facts may convince you of the need to keep your eyes open.

In one industry, catering and licensed premises, the loss rate is calculated to be 8 per cent! This might be higher than average, but the anecdotal evidence for theft of time and goods in industry and commerce is quite overwhelming.

Theft in retail stores, 'fiddling' of expenses, even the use of employers' telephones and stationery (if allowed to grow beyond what is reasonable) also represent losses.

Sixty per cent of the retail employees who responded to a recent University of Minnesota survey report they've stolen from their companies. Many sales clerks admitted to buying goods for friends and relatives with their discount cards, while increasing numbers of buyers and managers said they're padding their expense accounts.

Retail stores are not the only place where pilferage occurs. Roughly 30 to 40 per cent of the working population in the United States is a bad risk for handling a company's money, merchandise, and secrets. 'The trouble is that too many people take integrity for granted. Innocent until proved guilty is a meaningful and deep-rooted American principle. But it doesn't preclude the need to install effective theft deterrents and to take measures to track down dishonesty,' states one American report.

Security devices, no matter how effective, cannot stop the problem of employee dishonesty and cannot stop actual stealing of equipment and supplies. Strong preventive measures must be taken to deal with this problem.

Why are employees dishonest?

Studies suggest that an employee who feels mistreated is more likely to engage in 'spontaneous counter-productive behaviour'. An employee who was discovered making as many as 30 personal, long distance phone calls from the company excused his behaviour saying, 'The company hadn't given me a rise for two years. Plus, the few calls I made wouldn't make one bit of difference in their expenses.'

This employee didn't realise the total picture. His 30 phone calls may have taken between £50 and £100 per month from the company; now multiply that over two years, and factor in other employees partaking in the same practice, and the company could be in real trouble.

Another reason given by employees for dishonest practices is that 'everybody does it, even the senior company officials'. Padding invoices or switching hours from one contract to another may be seen by employees as evidence of the company's own dishonesty, giving them permission to do the same.

The exposure of slush funds and bribery used to obtain contracts, not to mention the insider dealings in major stock exchanges, have all contributed to a lowering of perceived business ethics.

It's easy to see how this environment creates easy rationalisations for employee dishonesty. Your employees will know the ethical climate of the company and follow the organisation's lead.

How to prevent employee dishonesty

The first step in preventing employee dishonesty is to create an atmosphere of honesty and ethical behaviour throughout the company. State all policies related to employee theft and dishonesty in your staff manual along with the steps that will be taken if the rules are broken. Then be sure that the illegal, unethical methods mentioned above are not practised in your company. Set the proper example.

Be reasonable when setting up your policies. For instance, almost every employee is going to use the photocopy machine some time or another. Recognise this, and create reasonable limits on its use. One company allows employees to make 30 photocopies a month. If employees need more, they bring in their own paper and make up to 200 copies without charge. A minimal fee is charged for over 200 copies. The employees have an incentive to be honest, knowing that the company is making provisions for them.

Employees caught breaking the rules must be immediately disciplined, no matter how high in the company structure. Explanations for your actions should be written out in a memo or company newsletter so everyone knows the rules are being followed and punishment will occur without exception.

Saul D Astor, an American security specialist, explains why the discipline is necessary, but sometimes difficult:

'Companies are reluctant to prosecute known thieves for a number of reasons. The crook may be a personal friend of the executive he reports to. . . . In some cases we run into the manager or supervisor caught stealing is so good at his job, the chief executive rationalises that it pays to keep him on despite his dishonesty. . . . The truth is that a hardnosed attitude and policy regarding dishonesty is the only morally feasible and economically practical approach to take.'

Dishonesty should not be shielded

Specific, tangible rewards can be created to encourage employees to report wrongdoing. To inspire those who would not want their names known, establish a box or area where employees can anonymously place reports on dishonesty. Create respect for the reporter, anonymous or not.

One company writes articles about its whistle-blowers without mentioning names, along with detailing the amount of money the company was losing in the specific case. There are some security measures of proven effectiveness.

Checklist 58

LOSS PREVENTION PROGRAMME

☐ Both management and sales employees, when engaged, view videotapes of past thieves being caught.

☐ Offer a substantial reward for a report of wrong-doing that results in the conviction or dismissal of the offender.

☐ It is a condition of employment to agree to inspection.

☐ There is a generous employee discount arrangement.

How to spot employee dishonesty

The following clues can be uncovered in your records to help spot employee dishonesty:

Checklist 59

DETECTING DISHONESTY

☐ Stock records and physical counts don't match.

☐ Control documents missing or out of sequence.

☐ Bad checks frequently accepted or approved by one employee.

☐ Unusual rise in consumption of supply items.

☐ Unusually high percentage of refunds or credits.

☐ Different figures on original and carbon copy of the same form.

☐ Erasures, changes, or pencil entries on forms that are not supposed to be altered.

☐ Substitute documents used excessively to replace 'lost' records.

☐ Employment record or references cannot be checked.

Signs in employee behaviour or actions include:

☐ Merchandise or materials missing from boxes or containers.

☐ Merchandise wrapped in a bag or package for no good reason.

☐ Something moved out of position between night and morning.

☐ Files or documents missing or out of place.

☐ Employee often carrying large bags or a stuffed briefcase.

☐ A sharp rise in the number of copies made on a photocopying machine or in the number of long distance phone calls.

What to do once you've discovered employee dishonesty

After you have discovered that an employee is stealing or abusing company privileges, obtain the best proof you can. For instance, keep detailed logs (as discussed in previous chapters) of an employee who continually comes into work late and leaves early. Have another supervisor verify this information.

Decide on the steps needed, following company policy. Does this employee deserve a probation period? (See Chapter 33.) How will an instant dismissal affect morale in the rest of your staff as well as overall productivity? Is a replacement readily available? These questions will also need to be addressed by you, because they'll follow closely on the heels of the action you take.

Next call the employee into your office and confront him or her with the evidence of dishonesty. Allow the employee to explain the actions, but make clear from the start of the interview that disciplinary actions will be taken. If you have decided to fire the employee, do so immediately, remaining firm and professional. (See Chapter 34, Facing Up to the Firing Task.)

Although you don't need to mention the disciplined or dismissed employee by name, use the action as reinforcement for other employees. Let them know why certain steps were taken. Be honest and forthright, and you'll retain the respect of the remaining staff.

Checklist 60

DEALING WITH DISHONESTY: SUMMARY

- [ ] Help to·prevent employee dishonesty by treating all employees fairly and creating an atmosphere of ethical behaviour. This is less costly and far easier than having to detect and punish dishonesty.
- [ ] Offer positive reinforcement for honest behaviour and whistle-blowing on unethical employees. This is another important preventive measure.
- [ ] Check all records and monitor employee's behaviour carefully if you suspect dishonesty.
- [ ] Obtain as much proof as you can of an employee's theft or abuse.

☐ Mete out punishment that is swift and sure.
☐ Publicise incidents and the resulting punishment.

Cracking down on dishonesty at all levels of your company will result in a better working atmosphere for all employees and decrease your losses.

In Chapter 33 we'll examine in further detail the steps involved in placing an employee on probation.

Putting an Employee on Probation

Employees will not always live up to your standards or the standards of the company. Even some good employees may have periods where their work is shoddy or where they may abuse company working hours, sick leave or holiday allocation.

This behaviour creates a drain on your company's resources. Other employees must work harder to handle overflow from a poor performer and can become demoralised. You must take action immediately.

There is a need for an early warning system which will alert management to potential problems while there is still time to do something positive about them.

Probation (not to be confused with the mandatory probation period for all *new* employees) is defined as a trial period or the act of granting continued employment on the promise of improved behaviour. It is a valuable management tool for the following reasons:

Checklist 61

A PROBATION PROGRAMME

- ☐ It gives employees clear feedback on their performance.
- ☐ Correctly worded, a probation gives the employee a goal that is measurable and attainable.
- ☐ It allows you to help a good employee over a troubled period without possible charges of favouritism.
- ☐ It minimises the trauma of dismissal if improvement in the work or attitude doesn't occur.

It should include the following elements:

- ☐ An unambiguous and clearly agreed definition of job responsibilities and performance expectations.

☐ A regular and objective monitoring of actual performance against agreed objectives and standards.

☐ An early signalling of emerging problems in the form of tangible, helpful 'feedback' to the individual.

☐ A review, by the individual and the supervisor, of the various problem-solving strategies available to them.

Discuss the problem openly

If you notice that an employee's work is not up to standard, first check that your perception of the employee's duties and responsibilities is the same as his or hers. A recent survey showed that over half of all superiors and subordinates didn't agree on most of the subordinate's required duties.

Solve the problem by having a clear, written position description. Take the time to go over the descriptions with each employee, answering any questions he or she may have. Ask employees to paraphrase the list of their responsibilities to check that you agree.

Although it will be time-consuming to go through this process, it will save you time and energy when an employee doesn't fulfil his or her responsibilities.

Once you notice a decline in performance or missed hours, bring it to the attention of the employee immediately. Hoping the problem will go away by itself will only make it worse. Call the employee into your office and firmly, but professionally, state the reasons for your concern.

Always criticise the behaviour, not the person. 'You've been at least one half hour late on 11 out of the last 12 working days. Can you explain this?' Offer the employee a precise assessment of his or her behaviour, along with the opportunity for explaining it.

As indicated earlier, you should document the poor performance as specifically as possible, using dates and times when appropriate. This provides evidence if you have to dismiss the employee later. It also helps to shape your efforts to improve the employee's performance.

This first discussion should be just that – a warning talk about the problem. Explain your judgement of the needed changes in the employee's attitude or behaviour. Then ask the employee to tell you the steps he or she intends to take to effect those changes. Set a time for a review of the needed changes, and hope the problem will be solved. If the employee's work does not improve, you will have to conduct a warning interview next. Summarise the discussion in a memo for your own files.

The warning interview

If appropriate, ask the subordinate to evaluate his or her performance since you first mentioned a problem. Many employees will recognise and admit they have not changed. Listen carefully, praising any straightforward admissions.

Explore options with the employee at this time. Is there a poor fit between the individual and the job? Could the employee do better in another area of the company? Can the job be restructured to create a better fit? Is dismissal of the employee a likely option? Discuss the alternatives, taking care to listen to the employee.

Some employees may become defensive. Bring out your evidence at this turn of events. Explain that the behaviour or attitude has not changed and that a memo summarising the warning interview will be placed in his or her personnel file. Give the employee a copy of the memo.

Explain the chain of events

Your company manual should clearly define a process for dealing with poor performance. First, the discussion; next, the warning interview; then probation; written warnings; and finally, if necessary, dismissing the employee.

This chain of events must be followed to the letter for all employees, no matter what the personal problems involved may be. Letting one employee exhibit poor performance or behaviour and not taking remedial steps may lead to decreased respect for you as a manager and an increased tendency among other employees to 'get away with it'.

At any time, if the employee's performance has improved, point out that you appreciate the change and would like it to continue.

Probation

If the performance has remained the same, or worsened, a formal probation is called for.

A formal probation involves the following:

Checklist 62

PUTTING EMPLOYEES ON PROBATION

- ☐ A written record of the performance or behaviour problem.
- ☐ A complete list of actions the employee must take to stay with the company.
- ☐ A prearranged time for the probation period.
- ☐ An understanding that dismissal is the only possible action if the goals are not reached.

If all else fails, the only alternative is termination. But the fired employee must know he or she was given an honest chance to succeed in the job.

The form on page 188 is an example of the documentation you need to include in a formal probation report. It may be needed if the matter ever goes to a tribunal.

Checklist 63

PROBATION CHECKLIST

- ☐ Establish a clear agreement about the duties and responsibilities of your subordinates.
- ☐ Have an open, warning talk with an employee whose behaviour or attitude is not up to par.
- ☐ If the talk was not enough, hold a warning interview, to be documented in the employee's personnel file. This interview should explore remedial action and support from the company for the employee to change his or her behaviour.
- ☐ Follow the chain of events leading to probation and then dismissal for all employees.
- ☐ Remember, probation is a formal action, with a specific time period and measurable goals to be reached during this period.
- ☐ Emphasise to the employee that dismissal is the only action that can be taken if the terms of the probation are not complied with.

If it comes down to having to fire someone, take heart. Few managers or supervisors relish the thought. Even fewer do it skilfully. Chapter 34 will walk you through how to face up to the firing task.

Figure 14

Employee probation report

Employee's name ——————————————————————

Division/Location ——————————————————————

Date of violation ——————————— Time of violation ————

Nature of violation
  Substandard work ——————————————————————
  Conduct ——————————————————————————
  Disobedience ————————————————————————
  Lateness ——————————————————————————
  Attitude ——————————————————————————
  Carelessness————————————————————————

Explanation for the violation
——————————————————————————————
——————————————————————————————
——————————————————————————————

Actions the employee has agreed to take during the probation period:
——————————————————————————————
——————————————————————————————
——————————————————————————————

Probation period: From ————————————— To ——————
Date employee was first warned of this violation ——————————

EMPLOYEE'S REMARKS

——————————————————————————————

Employee's signature ————————————————— Date ————

Signature of supervisor preparing report ———————————————

Title ————————————————————————— Date ————

CHAPTER 34

Facing Up to the Fear of Firing

Firing an employee is never easy. Looking someone in the face and saying that you no longer need his or her services is an emotional strain on you, on the person being fired, and can disrupt work in the rest of the organisation. In fact, managers frequently postpone dismissing an employee, even when it is absolutely necessary, to avoid the unpleasantness.

Most supervisors/managers have little experience of dismissing employees and horror stories about the employees' reactions (often somewhat exaggerated) abound. Additionally, the necessity of the firing involves admitting your own prior inadequate judgement or the poor judgement of your company in engaging the person.

Done quickly, but planned thoroughly in advance, firing an employee can have some positive aspects for you, your company, and the departing employee.

If you have already decided that an employee must be dismissed due to poor work, a disruptive attitude, pilferage, or some other reason, and have followed the steps in the previous chapter on giving the proper warnings and probation, answering the questions listed below will help you face up to the unpleasant task with as little discomfort and as much benefit as possible to you, your company, and the fired employee.

- ☐ Have you documented the reasons for dismissing the employee as well as the dates and steps taken to warn him or her of poor performance?
- ☐ How is the employee's presence affecting the morale of the rest of the staff?
- ☐ When is the best time of the day and week to tell the employee?
- ☐ What procedures should you follow in the termination interview?
- ☐ What positive aspects can arise for you, your company, and your former employee?

Document the problems

As stressed in previous chapters, it is vital to keep a detailed record of the problems you have faced with a particular employee. Did he or she have a habit of arriving late and leaving early? Do you have written records of daily time sheets? Was the employee found stealing equipment or resources from the company? Was this documented by another person in the company or an outside agency? Was the employee's work consistently not up to par? Can another supervisor verify your comments in writing?

Keeping such a record will come in handy if you are later challenged by the former employee or a union. It will also serve as a refresher for you when preparing for the termination session.

Also keep the details on warnings and probation with the date and method written down. For instance 'John Jones was warned verbally on 13 July 1986 about his lateness, a written warning notice (signed in acknowledgement by the employee) followed on 3 August, and he was formally put on probation on 31 August.' This information will track the progression of events, showing that the employee was fairly and properly warned about his or her behaviour and attitude, received adequate training and feedback, and had opportunities to transfer to another area of the company (if that was an option).

Recognise the effects on company morale

Delaying the firing of an unproductive (and possibly destructive) employee will not make the problem go away. Other employees are often more aware than you realise of the work habits and productivity of their fellow employees. They realise when someone is 'getting away with murder' and their own work may slip if they see shoddy work or work habits being tolerated.

Your staff wants to work for an effective, committed leader. They may regard your reluctance to dismiss an unworthy employee as evidence of your lack of respect for their good work as well as a lack of leadership. Delaying the necessary action diminishes your professional integrity, whereas taking control of the unpleasant situation, although it may initially create some misgivings among employees, will eventually result in the strong leadership employees expect and want.

Properly handled, done with dignity and poise, a dismissal can be an excellent public relations exercise, providing stimulation and relieving the tension of repressed hostilities. Your staff would rather believe you courageous than cowardly. They will respect and admire you for accepting the full burden of your responsibility as a leader. But if you dodge your duty, then you invite the sneaky suspicion that you are weak.

Timing the firing properly

Many feel that the best time to fire an employee is late Friday afternoon for the following reasons:

Checklist 64

TIMING THE DISMISSAL

- [ ] It provides an automatic two-day cooling off period for all involved.
- [ ] Other employees are busy thinking about their plans for the weekend and are not as likely to be affected by any unpleasantness of the situation.
- [ ] It gives the dismissed employee time to clean out his or her office immediately without the distracting presence of other workers.
- [ ] If necessary, it allows you to call a meeting first thing Monday morning, when your employees are ready to start the week, to explain the action.

(*Note*. There are also arguments for mid-week firings – a viewpoint not shared by the author.)

Procedures to follow

Avert any potential problems by checking the staff manual and contract of employment. Also check employment law with regard to notice and dismissal, and particularly compensation. Company handbooks can provide ammunition for a disgruntled employee.

If the person is in a high-level management position, there are other steps that may need to be taken. If the person has an employment contract, check with your company lawyer for prerequisites for dismissal and make sure you have the necessary grounds. Withdraw any signatory powers immediately and notify bankers, customers, and accountants that the person is no longer with the company and no longer has signatory powers. No additional explanation is necessary. Providing details may be seen as defensiveness on your part.

Have the employee hand over all keys, security cards, company material, and credit cards at the time of dismissal. Don't accept the excuse that the employee needs to get a key or security card from home and will bring it to the office later. Occasionally a disgruntled former employee has used a key to get into the office immediately after being fired to purloin company material or destroy company property. If need be, tell the employee you will despatch a courier to follow him or her home and pick up the missing items at once.

Make the break clean

Never fire an employee on impulse, but once you have thought out the action carefully and concluded that your company can no longer keep the employee, make the break clean.

Tell the employee that his or her services are no longer required, briefly state the reasoning that led to this decision, point out the warnings that were given previously, and emphasise that the decision is irrevocable.

Do not get into a long, involved discussion about the reasons for the dismissal at this point. Emotions are probably running high and an argument now will not benefit either you or the departing employee. Since being fired is a crushing experience, conduct the session with dignity. Any ego-boosting you can give such as 'I believe that with your natural enthusiasm you'll soon find employment that is better suited to you,' will be a kindness.

After collecting the necessary keys, credit cards, and company material, give the employee his or her final pay cheque with all holiday pay and any severance pay included. Be sure all the money owed to the employee is included in this last pay cheque. Don't skimp here as that may be cause for a tribunal appeal.

Positive aspects

It is important to remember that there can be positive aspects to a dismissal for you, the company, and the employee concerned. Employees being fired are frequently relieved. It couldn't have been pleasant for them to be under the stress of working in a bad situation. A researcher fired for a negative attitude confided that she hated her job but didn't have the courage to quit. The firing gave her the impetus she needed to make the career change she had wanted for quite some time.

You can point out that it is a new opportunity for the departing employee. If your company has an outplacement service be sure to give the employee all the necessary information about such a service at the time of dismissal. Firing an unproductive employee relieves you of an unpleasant situation and can be an opportunity for communication with the rest of your staff.

It depends on your management style, of course, but you could call a staff meeting for an opportunity to clear the air of any misconceptions that may have arisen and also as a training opportunity. Re-emphasise company policies, point out unacceptable behaviouur, and reinforce good attitudes and behaviour with praise.

Do not fall into the trap at this point of engaging in a discussion with the rest of the employees or allow them to put you on the defensive. Simply give them the facts, reinforce the proper behaviour, and end the meeting.

Checklist for firing

All companies, regardless of size, should have a form to be filled in by the supervisor and signed by the dismissed employee at the termination interview. If your company does not have such a form, use the one on the next page as a starting point, adjusting it where necessary.

Additionally, the following checklist will serve as a refresher before the termination briefing.

Checklist 65

THE DISMISSAL BRIEFING

- ☐ Was the employee fairly and properly warned about his or her work problems?
- ☐ Are the warnings and methods properly documented?
- ☐ Have you timed the interview to ensure that minimum distractions will occur?
- ☐ Have you followed company policies to the letter?
- ☐ Have your accounting and personnel departments prepared the necessary pay cheque and outplacement information?
- ☐ Have you prepared to keep the interview brief, dignified and on target?

Figure 15

Termination procedure

Employee Name ———————— Title ————————————

Department ———————————— Location ——————————

Date of termination ——————— Holiday due ————————

Employee has received:

    Final pay cheque ————————————— ——Yes ——No

    Holiday/severance payment ——Yes ——No

    Outplacement information ——Yes ——No

    Insurance information ——Yes ——No

Employer has received:

    Identification card ——Yes ——No

    Company credit card ——Yes ——No

    Repayment of any loans ——Yes ——No

    Keys ——Yes ——No

    Parking permit ——Yes ——No

    Office equipment ——Yes ——No

    Other (specify) ————————————————

Other comments: ————————————————————

—————————————————————————————

Signature of employee

Supervisor's signature   Date/Time

Firing an employee is not easy, but delaying the action from fear of its unpleasant aspects can hurt you, your company, and even the employee to be fired. Do it now and do it well!

CHAPTER 35

Helping the Battered Employee

A female employee phones up to report sick again. You, her boss, have had enough; it seems justifiable to get rid of her. Look again. She may be the one out of every three women who is physically abused by a spouse or lover. The statistics are overwhelming and a suburban housewife is just as likely to be abused as an inner-city woman.

Both women and men can be victims of batterers. This chapter will refer to females since they are more likely to be victims.

After reading this chapter you'll be able to answer the following questions:

☐ What form does battering and abuse take?
☐ What can you do to help the battered employee?
☐ Why is your taking the situation seriously of great importance to the employee?
☐ How can you detect signs of abuse?

Comes in many forms

The abuse takes many forms. It may be physical, emotional, or verbal. The abuser might punch, slap, kick, knife, or otherwise harm the woman; or he might threaten or harm the woman's children or relatives. An abusive partner will harass the woman at work, often turning up where she works in the hope that it will cause her to be fired. Then the woman would become more dependent on him, and he would be more in control of the relationship.

There are many types of abusers, all with excuses as to why they act the way they do. There is the 'Saturday night, I was drinking' abuser, the everyday assaulter who feels his wife is his property, the once-a-month 'I couldn't help myself' abuser, and the vengeful ex-husband or ex-boyfriend who swears 'I'll never let you go.' Usually the cause is deep-rooted. The abuser cannot tolerate himself so he acts out his anger on his intimate partner, accusing her of making his life unhappy.

At the workplace

A troubled employee may appear depressed or show fatigue, weight loss or increased use of tranquillisers or stimulants. She may seem preoccupied, be unable to concentrate or even display irritability.

What can you do as supervisor to help an employee you suspect is being abused?

First, you can understand what abuse is, including the cycle of battering. There is a pattern to most violence.

In the first stage, the tension-building phase, a woman tries to behave according to her partner's wishes, to keep the children quiet and make a good dinner. Unfortunately, she cannot control the situation. Only the abuser can control the violence, although he always blames the victim, accusing her of provoking him.

The second stage, the actual battering, may last anything from one hour to several days.

The third stage is the calm after the storm. It is difficult for people to understand this 'honeymoon' stage. Some abusers are sorry and behave almost like little children. Others are less conscience-stricken. While not overtly sorry, they are at least not actively wild. Usually the victim is grateful for this peace and hopes that it will continue. She may want to leave the abuser, but mindful of what that would mean – moving, changing the children's schools, job pressures, financial struggles, and family pressures from both her side and his – she stays. Therapists point out also that the 'security' of what is known, even if the woman is experiencing considerable abuse, is still preferable, often to the 'unknown', ie what will happen if she leaves.

Despite the victim's best efforts to keep her partner happy, the cycle of violence repeats itself. The tension builds up, actual abuse occurs, then for a short time there is peace.

The victim's job performance is naturally affected. At some point, she may admit to the problem she is having. At that point, as her boss, your responsibility is to take her seriously and to respect her fears.

Taking the situation seriously

Most abused women are afraid that they will not be taken seriously, that no one will believe them. Usually they tell their boss only after the partner's threats or acts of violence interfere with their performance at the workplace. The women no longer feel safe at work. Their partners may be phoning them at their job or visiting and making threats.

Obviously, a place of employment is not a fortress, but there are steps that a supervisor can take to provide his or her employees with protection from intrusion on the job. At the very least, visitors can be screened. If any employee has asked that her husband be kept away from the workplace, her request should be respected. The husband may play down the significance of the request, even charmingly laugh it off as a lover's quarrel, but his wife's concern should be taken seriously.

Detecting abuse

An observant supervisor may detect signs of a problem. For instance, employees who receive but do not make a lot of phone calls may be suffering from harassment. Similarly, women with high absenteeism records may not be unreliable but may be victims of abuse. They may be waiting for visible injuries like black and blue bruises or cuts to heal. They are ashamed of their situation and want to hide the evidence that shows their loved one beats them.

Also, supervisors should be on the look-out for female employees who seem 'accident-prone': women who often say, 'I had a minor car accident,' 'I tripped over the kids' toys,' and so forth. They may be covering up the assaults on their body.

Some supervisors are hesitant to approach an employee they suspect is being abused. After all, it might seem to the individual that they are butting into her personal life. But these same bosses will fire the woman for high absenteeism, and that will certainly affect her life.

Positive action

Without invading her privacy, it is possible to let an employee know that the company she works for is concerned. It's not inappropriate to discuss the woman's home life. As a supervisor, you might start off by telling the female employee, 'I'd like to help you keep your job; you seem to be having some problems. You're usually a good worker. I'm wondering what's happening? Are there some personal problems interfering? Can I help in any way?'

You may encounter resistance from the employee. She may not be ready to do anything. That, perhaps, is the toughest part of helping someone, knowing when to step back. You can offer your help and let her know that when she is ready, you will do what you can.

Here's a checklist of what you can do to help a battered employee:

Checklist 66

HELPING THE BATTERED EMPLOYEE

☐ Take time to understand the problem.
☐ Take the employee seriously when you are called upon.
☐ Show your support by asking if you can help.
☐ Safeguard the workplace from intrusion.
☐ Refer your employee to appropriate counselling services.

This concludes Part 5. Part 6, Handling Departing Employees, represents a shifting of gears. Chapters 36 to 39 examine the problems involved when a good employee wishes to depart.

Part 6

Handling the
Departing Employee

One of the many heartbreaks that a supervisor experiences over the years is the departure of a good employee. The phenomenon is increasing with each passing year. Despite high mortgage interest rates and housing problems, mobility increases.

Nevertheless, the fact that good employees depart frequently for greener pastures can be of little solace to the manager or supervisor in a small or highly specialised department who had come to rely on someone who consistently performed well.

Don't take it personally

It's important to remember that the departure of a good employee should not necessarily be taken personally. The employee is not so much leaving your department or your company as seeking greater opportunity, a new challenge (or as is often the case, the experience of being disappointed elsewhere).

It's a sad fact of contemporary society that the greatest increase in income that a worker can achieve is through a change in organisations rather than through an increase in compensation in the present organisation.

In the following chapters we'll look at:

- ☐ Clues for detecting the job seeker.
- ☐ Tips for inducing an employee to stay.
- ☐ Preventive and maintenance procedures for the impact of future losses.
- ☐ Guidelines for parting company effectively and gracefully.

CHAPTER 36

Detecting the Job Seeker

Way back in Chapter 5 you read about Walter Ross who was stunned when one of his employees, Harry Morris, abruptly resigned from the company. We learned in that chapter of the existence of built-in turnover factors which, if present, increase the probability that new employees will turn over much too quickly.

This chapter focuses on employees with whom you may have been working for several months, if not years.

When a good employee on your staff is actively seeking a job elsewhere, invariably there are several significant clues that will indicate to you what is happening long before the employee hands in the resignation note. It is important to know when a good employee is hunting for a new job and to be able to recognise the clues offered.

This chapter will enable you to answer the following questions:

☐ Why is it valuable to learn in advance of a potential departing employee?
☐ What changes in appearance may be noticeable?
☐ Is it appropriate to check up on employees who report sick?
☐ What office behaviour provides clues?
☐ What other subtle clues may betray the job seeker?

The inside score

The loss of a good employee's skills to your organisation represents an economic setback; your skilled labour or talent supply has been reduced. However, there are other reasons, perhaps of less significance, but nevertheless of some importance to total operations. For example, a good employee (or a bad one for that matter) may seek a new job while being financed through you. This does not imply that the employee is not doing the job, but that he or she may be 'coasting' on a previous fine effort and is in fact doing only the minimum necessary at present.

Linda Neuhaus, benefits co-ordinator for a major petroleum company observes, 'An employee's leaving for a presumed better job causes other employees to think that the grass may be greener elsewhere for them, too.' The departing employee may later provide new employment contacts for those who remain. Neuhaus says, 'Good employees know who else is good and who is ripe to be plucked from the organisation.'

Often, an employee's efforts do not affect the total operations until a week, two weeks, or sometimes a few months later. Thus, it is easy for some employees to coast for a significant length of time before leaving the old job for a new one. What are the clues that will tip you off far in advance that a good employee is job hunting?

Change in dress

A male employee who suddenly starts wearing three piece suits to work with a new overcoat, matching tie pin, expensive watch or other paraphernalia may be attending job interviews during lunch or getting up early in the morning and attending them before work (if he is seeking employment in the same city) or may be leaving work at 4.30 or 5.00 pm to head across town for a job interview.

Whether or not the employee normally wears a three piece suit, or a suit at all, the important 'tip off' is to look at the employee's shoes. Few good employees would ever enter a job interview with shoes that are unshone; however, many good employees often go to work each day with shoes that are unshone because they are secure in their present job and no one is really observing them critically each day.

If a female employee is job hunting, you may detect crispness in her hair style, shoes with a slight heel, and she may be carrying a brief case or some type of business folder that day, as opposed to the conventional hand bag. 'The female job seeker,' says Neuhaus, 'seeks a slimmer, taller appearance.' Women may also choose to wear 'a business suit, perhaps with a colour coordinated scarf or bow tie.'

Unfortunately, many times when employees have job interviews, that is the day that they choose to report sick, and thus no clues are provided concerning their dress or appearance.

If it is suspected that an employee is job hunting rather than home sick, it might not be a bad policy to get in the habit of calling personally to wish the employee better health, or to learn perhaps they 'just stepped out' at the moment you phoned. It's within an employer's right to phone occasionally when an employee is sick, at the very least to determine how the employee is feeling and when they think they might be coming back. This is not prying or playing 'Big Brother' because the employee is probably being paid for the day. As long as employees are being paid, you have a vested interest in ensuring that they are not getting a free ride.

Increase in clerical activities

Have you ever detected that one of your employees has been mailing a number of envelopes, or seems to have some sort of preoccupation with clerical activities when, in fact, clerical activities are not part of the employee's job? This may be a tip-off that they are job seeking. While most employees will mail CVs and do much of their 'homework' of the job search at home, often it is more convenient to send a few letters during the lunch hour or to post letters in town so they will arrive sooner.

Some employees may even begin to use the office typewriter and some of the plain stationery for their own purposes. It is very important to check the use of the office copier, as many job-seeking employees will use the copier to maintain a record of letters sent, or to copy other correspondence.

If you suspect that an employee is using office materials and appears to be more interested in some of the clerical activities, the best way to handle the situation is to approach the employee casually and ask the question: 'Is that for the XYZ report, or are these the exhibits for the study on DEF?' When asking such a question you will automatically force the employee to offer some type of explanation as to what the materials in question are. It is a mistake to ask employees *directly* what the materials are, because they may have mentally rehearsed what's going to be said if they are confronted with the clerical or office materials, and thus the answer will provide less information. Also, you may cause a confrontation. By using the recommended questions, an employee might be 'scared' out of working on, or with, these materials any further. They may then realise that they have a job to do for you, and they may think that nothing else was on your mind when you posed the question.

Avoidance of eye contact

It's almost a universal phenomenon that when good employees who have worked for you and participated in some of the major successes of the company are undertaking a job search, it becomes very difficult for them to look you in the eye on a sustained basis. In fact, as they grow closer to the time in which they believe that they are leaving, they generally try to keep eye contact as brief as possible or avoid it entirely. Be aware of this phenomenon of eye contact avoidance, particularly at staff meetings, and during one to one discussions with the employee.

If you suspect that the lack of eye contact is due to the employee's desire to leave the firm, you might ask if something is troubling the employee because he or she 'seems a little on edge'. The typical response will be of this nature: 'I just haven't been feeling myself lately', 'I'm a little tired these days' or 'Oh, I don't know.' If the employee does in fact give an answer that is similar to one of these three responses, there is a high probability that something is 'up'. If they give a direct answer that sounds like an accurate reason and you still suspect that they may be job hunting, you will have to look for other clues.

An excellent way to determine whether recent avoidance of eye contact is an indication of a planned departure, is to ask the employee out to lunch. Once again, if departure is planned, then lunch should prove to be a bit uncomfortable and they may offer some resistance, or perhaps postpone it for a few days.

Subsequently, you will be taking the employee to lunch and it is important to sit across the table so that the employee has no choice but to look at you. You might then discuss some of your plans and projections for the coming year and ask the employee how he or she feels, and how they may best fit in.

A job-seeking employee might have an extremely difficult time after such a question is posed and may refer to how the company may best achieve those plans, while not necessarily including themselves in the response. A typical response might be something that sounds like this: 'Well, I think the department could be doing a, b, and c and then after six months proceed to d and e.' Notice within that response there is no mention of what they personally might be doing, their level of participation, or anything at all that refers to themselves.

Increased telephone messages and time on the phone

If you walk past the receptionist's desk and notice, on a continuing and daily basis, that an employee suspected of job hunting has an inordinate number of telephone messages, this is a clue that a job search may be under way. If, when passing the employee's desk or office you happen to look in for a second, and see the employee on the phone repeatedly, though this is not a regular part of the employee's task or responsibilities, this is a signal that the employee may, in fact, be contacting prospective employers.

This is a bad situation for two reasons: one, company time is being used to undertake the job search, and two, even if the job search is not being undertaken, for whatever reason, the employee is using your telephone to conduct business that is not necessarily in direct support of your company. Although it is necessary to allow employees to use the phone and conduct their lives in the manner in which they choose (as long as they do a good job at work and are consistent with company policy and procedures) it is nevertheless undesirable to observe an employee making inordinate use of the phone.

A harmless question that might disarm an employee and yet is effective is: 'Is that G company calling about those shipments for Thursday?' or 'If that is Mr X, tell him about the meeting that has been moved up a few hours.' Regardless of an employee's phone-usage level, if, for any reason, you denote that the quality or level of effort applied to the employee's tasks and responsibilities is falling, it is time to take the employee aside and ask if there are any personal problems or if there is anything that you can do to help. At no time should an employee be allowed to have free reign at the office solely because you suspect that he or she may be job hunting and you are afraid that anything you may do will hasten the departure.

This is a common problem among small business owners and managers at all levels, because very few of us have had training in termination or parting procedures.

Other changes in behaviour

There are other minor, or less subtle changes in the employee's behaviour that may indicate that he or she is contemplating leaving the firm. One mode of behaviour is characterised by a slight cynicism regarding ongoing company goals or projects or those about to be undertaken. This cynicism will not usually be revealed at larger company meetings; however, it is more inclined to be revealed in small group settings, especially with colleagues and subordinates.

New-found personal organisation or neatness traits are also an indication that something may be stirring. Often an employee will start dismantling his files and reference materials in advance of his or her departure. Also, very often employees will throw out obsolete or irrelevant files or information so as not to clutter their desk or drawers, and symbolically their minds.

Another subtle clue and one that is rather difficult to recognise is the employee's use or overuse of the medical benefits provided by the company. In many instances, departing employees have decided to have that check-up that they have been meaning to have for some time. Some employees will also become acutely aware of the terms regarding company policies and fringe benefits so that they can obtain maximum value prior to their departure. Another minor clue is when an employee becomes acutely aware of the number of flexidays, leave days and sick days that have accumulated, and can be seen in conversation and consternation regarding exactly how much time has accrued.

It should be remembered that these behaviour traits, as stated above, are only minor clues to some of the major ones discussed previously, as many employees are acutely aware of their fringe benefits and often show great concern as to how much time or benefits have accrued to them. Nevertheless, a good employee who previously has not exhibited this behaviour, who is presently doing so, may in fact be contemplating leaving the company.

Here's a checklist of items that may tip off a job-seeking employee:

Checklist 67

DETECTING THE JOB SEEKER

☐ Change or improvement in dress and hairstyle.

☐ Increase in sick days used.

☐ Increase in clerical-type activities by non-clerical employees.

☐ Avoidance of eye contact.

☐ Increase in phone messages and usage.

☐ Display of mild cynicism or sarcasm regarding organisational goals.

☐ Improvement in personal organisation – desk, files, shelves.

☐ Interest in fringe benefits, amount of leave built up etc.

In the following chapter, ways to possibly induce a departing employee to stay are discussed.

CHAPTER 37

Inducing a Good Employee to Stay

Katherine Mathers was almost certain that her best staff member, Lisa Knight, was job seeking. All the clues were there, and worse, Lisa's pattern of absenteeism and reporting had shifted in recent months.

If you have detected several clues and feel very strongly that one of your employees is job hunting, and if you have a good rapport with the employee, take him or her aside and talk about it openly and honestly. It should be understood that we are all seeking to better ourselves and sometimes we have to leave a good position and a good company for a better opportunity elsewhere.

After reading this chapter you'll have a better understanding to answer these questions:

- ☐ What can you as supervisor ask of the job-seeking employee?
- ☐ Is it appropriate and/or useful to make a counter offer?
- ☐ Is it in order to counsel employees that are planning to depart?
- ☐ Why is a close encounter valuable in getting at the real issues?

Seek continued performance

If you can converse with the employee regarding the job search, as Katherine finally did with Lisa, there are certain fundamental requests as manager/supervisor that you can make. First, you can request that the employee steadfastly give 100 per cent effort while continuing to be employed in your firm, and can look forward to increases in pay and promotions, if, during the job search, their efforts merit such advances. You can also ask to be kept informed.

If an employee is presently speaking to several prospective employers but doesn't have a particular job in mind, there is nothing wrong in him or her telling you that he or she does not contemplate a move for at least another three to four months. This gives you much more information than if they contemplate leaving in 30 days, and allows you to counteract any job offer that the employee may receive.

With the good ones, counter offer

While it is not recommended for every employee, with some you may say, 'Come to me when you think you have got your best offer and we will talk about how I may be able to help you match it here.'

One owner/manager of an office supply distributorship offered this simple formula for retaining your best employees. 'Whatever they're offered at another company – match it! You'll both win in the long run.' Obviously, this is not a policy to be broadcast, but it does warrant consideration. Presenting a counter-offer allows you to talk to employees at the time when they are perhaps at the height of indecision. If the offer that they claim they have received is much more than you care to match, you may then decide that it's not worth keeping them, at that price. However, if the offer is in line with what you may be willing to advance them to, retaining the good employees may yield a far greater cost saving than the replacements you would have to find.

There is no question that many employers take very good employees for granted, and unfortunately never do begin to appreciate them until they realise that they are going to lose (or after they've lost) the employee (see Chapter 27, Undermining the Ideal Employee).

If your relationship with the employee is very well developed, you may even serve as a type of job counsellor for them. After all, you took them on in the first place, you saw skills and abilities that you felt could be used in your company, and very often you know their strengths and weaknesses better than they do.

It is not uncommon for an employee to depart from a job for a year or two, only to return. They too often recognise that your organisation wasn't so bad after all, or that there really were more opportunities for advancement with you than they had originally recognised. Or perhaps you have expanded your operation and they now visualise the ability to make a long-term sustained contribution to the future success of the department.

Close encounters

Periodically, sit down with employees on an individual basis and try to relate on a gut level. Relating at a gut level means asking an employee, for example, what's really on his or her mind, or 'how could we really improve things,' or any other type of question that elicits an emotional, deep-seated response. This type of encounter is excellent in developing a good working relationship – particularly with key employees – and for gaining more information relating to a key employee's quest to depart.

The point of this encounter is not to make the employee uneasy, but to try to prevent a good employee from leaving (if they are contemplating leaving and the situation is reversible). It could be that the employee doesn't want to leave and may have some personal problems or frustrations with which you may be able to help. Don't write off or give up on the good employee – often the desire to jump ship passes.

Here's a checklist of what can be done to induce a departing employee to stay or to ensure that the parting is mutually comprehended:

Checklist 68

INDUCING A DEPARTING EMPLOYEE TO STAY

- ☐ Request continued high performance.
- ☐ Ask to be kept informed.
- ☐ Try to get an advanced departure date.
- ☐ Explore making a counter-offer.
- ☐ Consider serving as counsellor to the employee.
- ☐ Arrange a close encounter.
- ☐ Don't give up on the good employee.

In the next chapter we'll examine both before and after measures to reduce the impact of the loss of a key employee.

CHAPTER 38

Reducing the Impact of Loss

Mark Thurston knew that Jerry Willis was leaving at the end of the month. Still, Mark spent no time finding a replacement or preparing for the disruption in work flow. Mark was too busy putting out the daily fires and was unrealistic in his approach to reducing the impact of the loss of Jerry, a key employee. Perhaps Mark thought 'things would take care of themselves'.

Act, don't react

Many supervisors believe that preparing for the loss of a key employee requires a defensive, even reactive, management style. This is not so. The flow of labour throughout business is a dynamic process and while some employees are particularly adept in handling given tasks and responsibilities, the distinct possibility exists that subordinates currently with the company can more than adequately fill the shoes of the departed employee.

What steps does the prudent manager take to minimise the disruption in operations when a key employee departs?

When a good employee departs, especially if it was on the heels of another departure or if it was on short notice, a typical response of a supervisor is to panic. This panic may take the form of revisions in policy procedures, issuing of memorandums, or conversely, light enforcement of organisational procedure in dealing with existing employees in the weeks and months to follow. All of these reactions represent poor management.

The overriding conceptual framework from which the supervisor's action should be derived is that employee supervision is basically sound, good employees will always be seeking opportunities elsewhere, the majority of employees will continue in the same productive manner, and, most importantly, new, good employees can once again be identified and recruited.

One accounting firm maintained a policy of honouring departing employees with a farewell luncheon. This did not accelerate their turnover rate and was a strong indication of the firm's relative strength and stability.

Rotating applicant file

The creation of a rotating applicant file is a necessity, even in the best of times. When you are fully staffed and everything is humming, the rotating applicant file must be maintained.

What is a rotating applicant file? This is a file of job applicants whom you have recently interviewed and with whom you must maintain contact for at least six to nine months. In other words, the wise manager should always be interviewing to gauge the quality and availability of human resources outside the organisation. Proper maintenance of the rotating applicant file means that even in the fact of a quick departure by a key employee, you'll have several potential applicants with whom you are already familiar to call upon.

This is so important. Think back to the time you engaged someone who either didn't accept the job at the last minute or departed after a few months. If you keep in touch with the more qualified applicants, you won't get caught short.

The easiest way to initiate the rotating applicant file is to establish a policy of continuous interviewing irrespective of immediate staffing needs. Then your staff will not be suspicious or anxious over the fact that for one or two hours every week you are conducting interviews.

Cross training

In college, most of us had a major subject area and a minor subject area. Why not apply the same principle to the organisation or corporate setting? For those employees who can handle the responsibility, schedule a few hours each week for them to gain experience in other tasks or in other departments. The schedule could be devised so that no department suffers a loss in person-hours, and the types of tasks and responsibilities offered need not significantly reduce overall productivity.

In the long run, cross training will in fact increase productivity as a network of employee skills is developed which serves as a counterbalance to the loss of any particular employee.

Vacation substitutes

Closely related to the strategy of cross training is the use of a key employee's holiday break to test others in the position. For example, if it is known that Bill Andrews is taking a one-week vacation at the end of October, plan to schedule one of your employees to take on some of Bill's tasks during that week. This process should be open and above board and explained in detail to the entire staff.

Take care to give the substitute assignments in which he or she can make a measureable impact during the substitution period and which will not cause the returning employee to undo or redo the same work. If handled properly, the use of holiday substitution can be of great benefit to all.

Sitting in on progress reports

Another strategy to strengthen your department and reduce the potential loss of a key employee is to invite staff periodically from other departments or with other responsibilities to meetings that the outside staffer might not otherwise attend. A variation on this theme would be to have outside staffers review reports, files and activities of other departments.

Again, the key to executing this technique effectively is to make sure that all employees are aware that this is company policy, and to minimise potential disruptions in personal and corporate productivity.

Wind up contingencies

Another strategy for reducing the potential impact due to loss of a key employee requires only a simple exercise which can be done at your desk in a matter of minutes. On a blank piece of paper write at the top 'What would I do if Terry Wright resigned today, leaving at the end of the month?'

You can fill in the name of anyone in your department, but this exercise is particularly useful when doing so for key employees. Now under that lead question, list all of the contingencies available or which might become available if the employee were to leave. The available options will vary widely from company to company and from department to department.

Some options may include placing an ad in the trade/professional journal, soliciting the talent of competitors, promoting from within, abolishing the position and reorganising the department, calling upon applicants in the rotating applicant file, or soliciting the opinions and advice of upper management. The point of this exercise is to illustrate that (1) there are options available and (2) only a minimum of preparation is needed to reduce the impact when a key employee departs.

Checklist 69

REDUCING DEPARTURE IMPACT

☐ Remember that it is the nature of the workplace for people to move on to new challenges and opportunities.

☐ Act, don't react. Remain calm and do nothing drastic.

☐ Establish a rotating applicant file.

☐ Provide or secure cross training for your staff whenever possible.

☐ Use vacation substitutes to facilitate cross training of employees.

☐ Encourage other supervisors to allow staff to sit in on meetings of other departments

☐ Speculate what you'd do if a key employee departed suddenly. Make a list of contingencies.

Chapter 39, the final one in this section, focuses on parting company effectively and gracefully.

Parting with Grace

D-Day is coming at the end of the month. One of your most productive staff members has accepted a job elsewhere. You tried all the suggestions in Chapter 37, and undertook all of the contingency planning suggested in Chapter 38. Is there anything else you should do before the final departure?

Yes.

If a good employee is leaving and you know it, and if the two of you have spoken and it is not possible to keep him or her from going, there are steps that can be taken to ensure that the parting is as professional and amicable as possible. Some supervisors use these final days to belittle, ignore or unfairly burden the departing employee, as if trying to get even. None of these actions is recommended.

Let's examine the steps that should be taken when you know that a good employee is departing, and help you to answer these questions:

- ☐ Why are letters of resignation nevertheless useful to obtain?
- ☐ Will a departing employee provide greater information at an exit interview?
- ☐ When should an exit interview be held?
- ☐ Do departing employees serve as ambassadors of you and your organisation?
- ☐ Why is it important to keep the door open?

Obtain letter of resignation

Requiring a departing employee to submit a letter of resignation is partially helpful in obtaining underlying causes for the departure. The 'partially' is because many employees will choose to be diplomatic when putting anything down on paper that will become a part of their permanent record with the company. The resignation letter, nevertheless, is valuable because it may provide a relatively brief and focused review of the employee's situation.

Virtually all mid- and upper-level management positions in business and industry carry an unwritten mandate which requires a written letter of resignation when departing. You are encouraged to obtain such a letter from *all* departing employees.

The resignation letter in itself represents an important exercise for the departing employee; perhaps he or she hasn't fully crystallised on to paper the reasons for departure. The resignation letter also serves as a good starting point from which to begin the exit interview.

Exit interview

Conduct an exit interview to determine precisely the reasons why each employee departs. Once a final decision to go is made, an employee will be more inclined to give you precise information about the reasons for leaving. This information is extremely valuable to you as supervisor because probably no one else will ever provide this type of information while employed.

It is important to remember that the departing employee is also an ambassador to, or of, your organisation, whether you wish them to be or not. At one time or another, they are going to be relating their experiences at your company with colleagues, relatives, friends etc. Even if they had encountered several months of rough going for any particular reason, if the parting was amicable, they will be more inclined to speak favourably about the organisation.

The exit interview should be held on the very last day, before an employee departs. The interview must be held in an atmosphere in which the employee and supervisor can calmly and quietly discuss the reasons for the departure. As noted, the resignation letter may not include all facets of the situation and the employee may relish the opportunity to present additional verbal commentary.

Many organisations use some type of exit interview form for the departing employee to fill in as part of the exit interview. See the example in Figure 16.

If there is reasonable evidence that the departure was due to a soured relationship or friction with management, it is wise to remember that the delicate balance of personal chemistry between management and staff is dynamic in nature – ever changing and evolving. Also, the old adage 'You can't please everyone' is especially true concerning employee relations. Employees seeking reasons for discontent will always find them.

The exit interview should not be used as a last ditch effort by management to convince the employee to remain with the firm. Any tactics of

Figure 16

Exit interview

Please rate these statements according to your experience or opinion
(5 = Best).

_ You were delegated sufficient responsibility.
_ Your work was praised and appreciated.
_ There were enough promotional opportunities.
_ Your job challenged you.
_ You had the opportunity to use many of your abilities.
_ You were encouraged to make suggestions or improvements.
_ You felt free to make a complaint or grievance.
_ You were supervised too closely.
_ You understood the company benefit programme.
_ You were satisfied with the working conditions.
_ You were given clear-cut directions.
_ You understood how your work fitted with other work in the organisation.
_ You were asked to do too much.
_ You felt underpaid for the work that you did.
_ You generally knew where you stood and got sufficient feedback.
_ Your supervisor was well organised.
_ You received valuable on-the-job training.
_ You disliked your job.
_ You feel this is a good place to work.

Please make any other comments on the reverse side.

this nature should have been attempted far in advance of the actual day of departure – one reason is that there is simply too much pressure on the employee on the last day to go ahead with the planned departure.

Even the world's best offer presented by management during the exit interview would be to no avail as management's integrity would be undermined in making such an offer.

Keep the door open

All the points stressed in this and the previous three chapters lead to the notion that it is necessary to keep the door open – let the departing employee know that, for now, it is understood greater opportunity may lie elsewhere. However, things do change (and quite frequently in contemporary society) and, combined with the experience the departing employee will gain with other firms in other positions, and new opportunities that may arise with your company in the coming years, it may be highly desirable to reassess and rediscuss the situation one, two or three years hence.

An employee who is both good and smart will acknowledge the professional courtesy that you have provided in keeping the door open and in not too long a time may take you up on your offer.

There is one more fundamental reason to make the parting of good employees as pleasant as possible: they worked for you and they probably helped you to reach your goals, improve your department or make a profit, and although you may not have recognised it at the time, your relationship was prosperous.

Checklist 70

CHECKLIST FOR GRACEFUL PARTING

- ☐ Do not belittle, ignore or unfairly burden a departing employee during the remaining time on board.
- ☐ Obtain a letter of resignation.
- ☐ Conduct the exit interview on last day.
- ☐ Find a quiet, calm setting.
- ☐ Use an exit interview form to gain additional information.
- ☐ Avoid trying to persuade the employee to stay.
- ☐ Keep the door open.
- ☐ Reflect on the prosperity of the relationship.

Does it hurt to let the good ones go? Of course it does. Should the departure represent setback to you or the organisation? No.

This concludes Part 6. In Part 7 we'll examine a very important aspect of your career – managing it!

Part 7

Managing Yourself

Time was when faithfully executing the responsibilities of your job was all that seemed necessary to ensure that your career advanced at a rapid pace. This is not so today and in many ways has really never been true.

In order to succeed as a successful manager/supervisor in the 1980s and 1990s, you must realise that you need to manage your career as vigorously as you do your staff. The concluding chapter of this book examines how to facilitate career advancement strategies.

Although you may not consider yourself a salesperson, much of what you do on the job and certainly much of what would be needed in future positions requires you to develop persuasiveness and selling skills. The value of getting qualified, breaking into print, joining with a mission and speaking to gain visibility are all also examined and help provide a blueprint by which you can outdistance the pack and increase your promotability.

Tips are also offered on researching your professional needs and mastering your professional reading which provide you with the winning edge.

Maybe you have never considered career self-management as a necessary, useful and continuing responsibility. After finishing this section it is hoped that you'll realise just how important it is and will have the necessary guidelines with which to begin.

CHAPTER 40

Honing Your Professional Skills

Honing your professional and interpersonal skills in the context of supervising for success entails face-to-face discussions with your staff, peer groups, boss and top management.

In managing your own career, it is important never to lose sight of the notion that 'selling' – communicating and persuading, and gaining exposure are valuable, almost mandatory skills for advancement.

This chapter will help you to answer the following questions:

- [ ] What is personal image?
- [ ] How can getting qualified help your career?
- [ ] What are some of the advantages of being published?
- [ ] Are there benefits in joining local associations?
- [ ] What are some key sources for researching information needs?
- [ ] Can you master that growing pile of reading material?

One key to a successful career is having a firm conviction of your own capabilities. This starts with a proper frame of mind. You may have superior supervisory and technical capabilities to offer, but this alone is not enough. Belief in yourself is transmitted to colleagues and associates above and beyond what you say. And as prolific business author Herman Holtz says, 'If you don't believe in yourself, who else will?'

In control and with awareness

The manager/supervisor in control and with awareness knows each day and each week what he or she will be doing, and knows the same about the staff being supervised. This person takes the time to review strategies and approaches supervision in a controlled and effective manner. This type of professional knows that taking the time to maintain personal control maximises presentation effectiveness and overall use of time.

The effective supervisor is eager to learn or read about new supervisory techniques. Also, he or she recognises that the time invested in keeping the car tuned up, the office and files in shape, and the wardrobe sharp pays dividends. This person welcomes luck but doesn't count on it, knowing that a well-executed, sustained professional effort is the best road to promotion.

Your personal image

Image has been defined as the sum total of all of the perceptions others have about you and your capabilities. Every element of your job over which you have discretion will contribute to the development of an image. If that image is solidly developed and consistently displayed, the task of influencing your staff and upper management will be greatly enhanced.

Your organisation expects certain behaviour and characteristics of professionals in your field. Within this area of expectation, however, it is recommended that you develop your own unique image, for this is what will differentiate you from rivals. For example, the supervisor who has a black belt in karate, or who recently visited South America, can cultivate a unique image based partially on the outside interests.

Here's how to hone your selling professional skills:

- [ ] Remember, everyone lives by selling something.
- [ ] Have a firm conviction in your capabilities.
- [ ] Maintain personal control and awareness.
- [ ] Cultivate your personal image.

Get qualified

Increasingly, professional qualification is regarded as a necessary component of a successful professional career. The number and variety of qualification courses available in all industries grows each year.

Many professional societies allow you to use the designation 'affiliate' while you are earning certification. Thus, as an affiliate, you can have the benefits of certification even before you complete the process. As a supervisor you can add to your professional credentials by seeking out and obtaining certifications that will enhance your reputation and standing in your organisation.

Breaking into print

You can enjoy a large number of benefits when you have an article printed in a business or professional publication.

The primary benefits of getting published include the following:

☐ Establishing your professional credentials.
☐ Creating a favourable impression.
☐ Bolstering your self-marketing efforts.
☐ Being invited to speak to groups.

The best topics for articles are derived from the successful work that you have already done. This may include reports, papers, summaries, guides and exhibits etc that you previously prepared which can be generalised and applied to a larger audience.

Here's a checklist of ideas for generating article topics:

☐ Make a list of job-related problems and ways to redress the situation.
☐ Make a list of new developments in your profession.
☐ Start a cuttings file of articles that interest you.
☐ Make a list of six, eight or ten ways to do something better.
☐ Recall your favourite professional experience, most unforgettable character, biggest disappointment etc.

Speaking to gain visibility

If the mere thought of speaking before a group makes you quiver, then skip to the next section. For you brave souls, many local organisations as well as civic and charitable associations actively seek speakers. Yet the social secretary of these groups must often scramble to find an interesting speaker. As a volunteer speaker to local groups, you enjoy many benefits including: improving your presentation skills, enhancing your CV, gaining community and professional exposure and increasing personal confidence.

Your decision on whether to seek speaking engagements as a career advancement strategy hinges on your ability to be interesting and have something worthwhile to say to a group composed of selected targets. If you've never spoken before a group, you have a unique experience in store. Everyone is nervous at first, but in a little while you may find it quite exhilarating.

Joining with a mission

How can joining outside groups help your career?

Earning a position of leadership in a high visibility organisation is an excellent way to be of service and, as a by-product, enhance your career potential. By volunteering your services and assisting civic and charitable organisations, targets of opportunity (those that may provide your next job!) come to know you as a person and then feel comfortable in discussing their business problems with you.

Civic organisations such as the Chamber of Commerce, Rotary, residents' associations, PTA, and civic groups afford business leaders and professionals ample opportunity to rub elbows with other key community and business leaders and jointly work on solving local, civic, public and business problems. When gaining personal exposure, it is assumed that you are fully competent in your profession and a rising star in the community.

Memberships of professional and civic groups should constantly be evaluated to determine whether career advancing activities, in addition to personal satisfaction, are being realised. Otherwise, joining can be a drain on your time and energy.

For the supervisor on the rise, these groups offer you a chance to gain a measure of visibility that most of your peers and colleagues will never know.

Mastering your reading

If you're like most business professionals, the odds are you can't keep pace with all the information that passes your way and may be necessary to absorb in pursuit of your supervisory efforts and towards the advancement of your career. In this 'age of information', most business professionals are experiencing information overload.

Successful managers/supervisors of the 1980s and 90s must be able to supervise their staff effectively, remain goal-oriented and yet stay attuned to the latest developments within the industry, advancing technology, and the field of management and supervision.

Active reading – seeking out those key publications and sources of information that supply you directly with what you need to know, is far preferable to passive reading – reading those publications such as the daily paper, general interest periodicals and a variety of direct mail materials you may receive which may take more time than they're worth.

If you haven't yet mastered skimming, it's still not too late to learn. Skimming involves perusing the first one or two sentences of a paragraph within an article to see if the information within that paragraph is pertinent to your immediate quest.

Skimming can also be used when confronted with several journals or periodicals at the same time. The basic pay-off to skimming is that it enables you to quickly determine whether or not you should invest any further time in the article or the publication at hand.

Scanning is a technique used with large volume materials. If you must research several books or periodicals for the purpose of extracting key information, scanning enables you to handle the task effectively in a short time. Scanning involves reviewing the table of contents, index, list of diagrams and tables, and occasional paragraph heads.

Reading at your desk

Surprisingly, many supervisors feel guilty about reading at the office desk. The guilt seems to stem from the fact that reading at the desk doesn't appear to be very productive and it certainly doesn't cause one to perspire. Many erroneously believe that if they're not seen in some form of motion then they're not really working or, worse than that, it appears to others that they're not really working. If this is a problem for you, you may wish to discuss the need to read at the desk with your boss and with your staff.

Reading can be delegated!

Though you may not have considered it previously, a stack of periodicals you've been wanting to get through, those key chapters in the latest book, or those reports that have been piling up, don't have to be read by you at all. They can be delegated to any of your staff including the most junior.

All that's necessary to delegate some of your reading workload effectively is to provide clear instructions as to what you're looking for and how you want it to be presented.

Here's a quick review for mastering your reading:

- ☐ Redefine precisely what your reading needs are.
- ☐ Practise skimming and scanning.
- ☐ Read at a desk.
- ☐ Delegate reading assignments to your staff.
- ☐ Explore database services.
- ☐ Reduce your reading time by using your ear – listening to cassettes.

Your career in perspective

Successfully managing your career involves time and effort and simply can't be left to the whims of fortune. The extra effort you put into advancing your career should be looked upon as a long-term investment.

The way to rise above the crowd is by not following it. Your two-pronged attack – successfully executing the responsibilities of your present position, and taking the extra steps to ensure your personal and professional development, should continue to be regarded as of equal importance. If you're willing to trust your instincts, carve your own path, and assume the risk of leadership, a spectacularly successful, rewarding career can be yours.

Management Reference Books and Further Reading from Kogan Page

Be Your Own Company Secretary, A J Scrine, 1987

British Qualifications, annual

The Business Fact Finder, ed Hano Johannsen, 1987

The Business Guide to Effective Speaking, Jacqueline Dunckel and Elizabeth Parnham, 1985

The Business Guide to Effective Writing, J A Fletcher and D F Gowing, 1987

The Business of Data Processing, Roger Carter, 1984

Business Rip-Offs and How to Avoid Them, Tony Attwood, 1987

The Business Writing Workbook: A Guide to Defensive Writing Skills, Ian Stewart, 1987

Choosing and Using Professional Advisers, ed Paul Chaplin, 1986

Don't Do. Delegate! The Secret Power of Successful Managers, James M Jenks and John M Kelly, 1986

Finance and Accounts for Managers, Desmond Goch, 1986

Going for Growth: A Guide to Corporate Strategy, Michael K Lawson, 1987

A Handbook of Computer Security, ed Keith Hearnden, 1987

A Handbook of Management Techniques, Michael Armstrong, 1986

A Handbook of Sales and Marketing Management, Len Rogers, 1987

How to Be a Better Manager, Michael Armstrong, 1983

How to Organise Effective Conferences and Meetings, David Seekings, 3rd edition, 1987

Improving Results from Business Entertaining, Melvyn Greene, 1986

International Dictionary of Management, Hano Johannsen and G Terry Page, 3rd edn, 1986

Managerial Moxie: A Basic Strategy for the Corporate Trenches, Lance H K Secretan, 1986

A Manager's Guide to Patents, Trade Marks and Copyright, John F Williams, 1986

Managing with Information Technology, Eric Deeson, 1987

Never Take No for an Answer: A Guide to Successful Negotiation, Samfrits Le Poole, 1987

Personnel Management: A Handbook for Employers and Line Managers, Michael Armstrong, 1987

Practical Sponsorship, Stuart Turner, 1987

ESSENTIAL MANAGEMENT CHECKLISTS

The Practice of Successful Business Management, Kenneth Winckles, 1986
Readymade Business Letters, Jim Dening, 1986
Sources of Free Business Information, Michael J Brooks, 1986
So You Think Your Business Needs a Computer?, Khalid Aziz, 1986
Winning Strategies for Managing People: A Task Directed Guide, Robert Irwin
    and Rita Wolenik, 1986
A User's Guide to the Manpower Services Commission, Alastair Thomson and
    Hilary Rosenberg, 2nd edn, 1987

Send to the publisher at 120 Pentonville Road, London N1 9JN for a full
list.

Index